Ben Whately

Black Dragon River

Published by Ben Whateley 2005

To Natalia

Chapter 1

I felt helpless and very alone. I was wide-awake; it was only 6am, but there were no curtains and the sun had been up for an hour. I lay in bed, staring vacantly at the sheet of plastic that covered the window, and wondered what I should do next.

I had come to Qiqihaer to learn Chinese, and, more importantly, to try to make some sense of the mystery of "China." Qiqihaer is the second city of China's far north-eastern Heilongjiang province in what used to be called Manchuria. Five and a half million Chinese live there, but because there is nothing ostensibly of the slightest interest either for tourists or for businessmen in the city, very few non-Chinese ever visit, and even many Chinese have never heard of it. From the distant comfort of my flat in London, my pretentious imaginings had seen it as the perfect place to try to discover the 'real' China; now that I was actually there, it seemed like a miserable, confusing and very cold concrete wilderness.

I looked back at my watch. I had managed to while away another eight minutes. Just how exactly was I supposed to start my 'discovery' of China? I had rather assumed that, having left family and friends behind and struck bravely out on my own, the rest of my plan should just take care of itself. I returned to pondering the plastic sheet and started feeling sorry for myself. At around eleven thirty, nature finally gave me the motivation I needed to move: I was ravenously hungry. I grudgingly wrapped myself up as warmly as I could, given that in a moronic fit of bravado before leaving London, I had left behind most of my warm clothes, and set off into the unending greyness of the city. For some reason I was surprised by how cold it actually was. I knew that it would be about -30°C, but somehow I hadn't really registered just how cold that would feel. My eyes were streaming, and the tears froze on my cheeks and eyelashes. Through my blurred vision, I tried to make out a shop that might be a restaurant, but all I could see was row after row of brightly coloured meaningless squiggles above every entrance. The windows were all iced up, so I couldn't see inside, and I was feeling too shy and fragile to just burst in to each shop in the hope that it was a restaurant. After just three minutes, my 'discovery' of China was already faltering badly.

I walked on for another twenty minutes, exploring my new neighbourhood. There were two wide boulevards lined with bare trees and concrete apartment blocks. Scattered between these there were more painfully uninspiring buildings surrounded by what would become, when finally the temperature did creep above freezing, muddy tracks. There were very few cars. Traffic consisted of a handful of bicycles and tricycles and the odd cart drawn by a mule. The occasional pedestrian hurried past, wrapped up in thick blankets and army surplus coats, keen to get back inside.

I had almost given up hope of ever finding lunch, when I finally spotted a photograph of food hanging above a dingy doorway. I rushed in, realising that in a few moments I would be too cold to move. I sat down and reached for the Lonely Planet phrasebook that should have been in my pocket. To my horror, I discovered that I had left that little lifeline back in my room. I should have given up there and then, knowing that I would now be unable to communicate, but I was too proud to admit my hopelessness, and too hungry to leave empty handed. So I grabbed myself a menu and set about ordering.

An uninformative exchange with the waitress followed, after which she gave up on me and called over a smiling man from the next door table who exceeded her in patience, if not in actual communication ability. I tried some elaborate mimes whilst I racked my brains for the name of just one dish. I noisily slurped down imaginary bowls of soup, I drew noodles in the air (in hindsight, a singularly unhelpful piece of mime) and I threw out the few words of Chinese that I knew, in the forlorn hope that they might correspond to a local delicacy. I toyed with the idea of picking things at random from the menu, but most of what I could see the other people in the restaurant eating looked too frightening to contemplate.

I needed time to think, so I decided to retreat, and order a cup of tea. 'Tea' in Chinese is 'Cha,' which has now come into the English language as 'a cuppa *char*,' so I felt fairly confident that I could manage to order it.

"Cha" I said, but he just looked confused, and then smiled still more broadly and inanely. "Cha, cha" I tried again, "cha cha cha cha-cha-cha!" I continued, getting a little louder and a little more desperate with each repetition, and at last he disappeared off. Rather disconcertingly though, he disappeared off out of the restaurant and away down the road. I was a little put out, but I waited patiently and tried to look in control; there was nothing else I could do. My patience was rewarded when presently he returned, and although the tea was nowhere in evidence, he brandished a handful of meat kebabs. I was getting more hungry by the minute and decided not to complain. The kebabs were covered in cumin and other spices and tasted smoky and delicious. I wolfed them down and the edge was taken off my hunger, but I wasn't quite sated. I then had the good fortune to see the waitress passing by with a large bowl of noodle soup; just what I was after. I pointed excitedly; "wo ye xiang! Wo ye xiang!" I gushed, which I hoped meant, "I also want! I also want". She looked a little bemused, but scuttled off and soon brought me back something completely different. And impressively disgusting. Having been so keen, I felt obliged to put on a bit of a show of eating it though, and shovelled about half of it down, using the old 'swallow before you have time to taste it' technique. I paid the paltry bill, and made my way back out into the street, followed by the smiling kebab man. He was jabbering away at me in the manner of one who had clearly learned nothing about my lack of language skills from our relationship thus far, but I tried my best to look friendly. After a few more incomprehensible grunts and wild gestures, I eventually understood what he was saying; he was holding a cigarette lighter out to me and encouraging me to take it. I tentatively extended my hand, and he pressed the lighter into it, nodding excitedly and beaming. I too nodded wildly, smiled broadly, and made off back to the university with a spring in my step, the cloud of my loneliness temporarily lifted by the kindness of a stranger.

Chapter 2

When I arrived back in my room I found a note from Mr Guo pinned to the door. Mr Guo held the dubious title of foreign affairs director of Qiqihaer University, and was a pushy little man of about fifty. He had picked me up from the airport in Harbin and taken me on the three-hour train journey back to Qiqihaer. Almost as soon as he had met me, he had started asking me in his abrupt English if I would like to teach at a middle school. I didn't. Not remotely. But he was the only person that I knew within about a thousand miles, and I didn't want to disappoint him. So I had agreed that I might go and visit the school at some time in the future, just to see if I was interested. The note told me that he would come at eight the next morning and take me straight there. A part of me was glad that I could now be certain that I would at least speak to someone the next day, but mostly I felt irritation at his pushiness, and dread at how I was going to make myself say 'no'.

As I slurped down my breakfast bowl of pot noodles the next morning, I thought about it more, and decided that I was simply being pathetic, and needed to assert myself a bit more. I wouldn't let them walk all over me: I was there to learn Chinese and I had budgeted so that I could spend all my time studying and waste no time taking distracting jobs. I wouldn't let my plans be derailed on my second morning by my inability to disappoint people. As soon as he arrived I would make it clear to him that I couldn't do the job.

Or so I told myself. But I hadn't expected him to turn up in such style. A black Cadillac (not a real one, of course, but a locally made Chinese copy) with tinted windows and a graceful silver statuette on the bonnet rolled into the yard in front of the dormitory and a uniformed chauffeur leapt out and opened the door to me. For a moment I didn't realise who it was, but then Mr Guo's combed-over head popped out and ordered me to get in. I paused for a moment, startled, and by the time I had composed myself enough to try explain to him that I didn't want to come, he had disappeared back inside. I bent over to speak to him, but by now he was shouting into his mobile phone, and just beckoned to me in irritation. It was clear that I was going to have to go with him.

And so it was that I gained my first insight into the Chinese education machine. The school building itself was an enormous concrete block with a traditional style Chinese roof stuck on top as a cursory nod to five thousand years of civilisation. Outside in the playground a regiment of children, all togged up in a hotchpotch of anoraks and woollen hats, were being paraded up and down. A beaming PE teacher was barking English commands at them in a strict tone. As one the grid of children responded to English commands of "attention!" "at ease" and "eyes right" (they all turned to the left). Chuckling to myself, I was ushered inside whereupon Mr Guo, the only other English speaker present, promptly took another call on his mobile phone and was indisposed to act as interpreter for the next twenty minutes. I was shepherded around the first floor in a bemused haze, peeking in at the occasional classroom, before being pushed up to the next floor. Here I assumed that I was in for more of the same, and busied myself with making the "oohing" and "ahhing" noises that I felt the situation required, when suddenly the door to one of the classrooms was flung open, just as I was mid-"ahhh". Forty little faces looked up in unison, just in time to see me stranded in a position of undignified terror, half way between a curious "ahh" craning over to peek through the tiny window, and a shocked "whhaagh?" as I sharply recoiled, and the realisation dawned on me that I was going to be expected to put on some sort of show for this sea of intimidating little moon faces. I then promptly did the only thing I could do to make the situation worse, and walked into the side of the opening door. Having thus caused myself extreme pain, the class extreme hilarity, and those showing me around unconcealed embarrassment, I entered the lion's den. In a trice, the easy laughter of the moment before vanished, as a stern and beefy girl at the front barked "stand up!" and the class immediately obeyed.

More orders were issued and the class chimed some nonsense in unison, before being instructed in the same military tone to be seated once more. Feeling a little like Bertie Wooster giving a speech at that girls' school, I gave a cheery "hello" through which I intended to show that I was friendly and likable, and that I had found the whole walking-into-the-door incident just as funny as they, and yet I was also a serious and intelligent teacher who demanded – and got – respect. The result, I knew as soon as the word was out of my mouth and my goofy two-handed wave was beyond the point of no return, was far more 'Bertie Wooster' even than I had feared. I tried to steady the boat with a couple of lively questions to the class, intimating that I was still very much in control, but the situation only worsened. Each question in turn fell on deaf ears; they lacked either the understanding or the inclination to answer. My voice started to quaver and my face burned red. Who knows how long this painful farce may have continued had not a lone bright spark from the team behind me stepped in and dragged me (a tasteful show of reluctance is always important) to the safety of the corridor.

Next I was shown into a sort of staff room which, I deduced from an 'English the staffroom' banner over the door, was the hang out of the English speakers. Somewhat reassured for a moment at the possibility of some English banter, I stepped boldly in, and found the teachers cowering in a corner petrified, no doubt, that their ruse of pretending to be able to speak English was about to be smoked. I did my best to coax them out with some friendly "hellos" of the sort used by nursery schools teachers separating bashful children from their mothers on the first day of school, and, at last, they ventured into the centre of the room. With my confidence on the rise, and egged on by the team, I tried a few questions on them. Things didn't go well. For their sakes, I did my best to pretend that I understood what they were saying, and that their answers were in any way relevant to my questions, but I'm not sure of my success. Running low on acting skills, I asked what level the students were at, and affected an interest in seeing some of the teaching materials. Mercifully this was understood, and the books were produced. I was thus able to legitimately lose a few minutes thumbing through the pages and furrowing my brow. I have to say the standard was exceptional; the comprehension passages were written in a verbose style delighting in a number of clauses, sub clauses and superfluous subjunctives that even I was a little wary of. It seemed extraordinary that these teachers could possibly do these exercises themselves, let alone teach others how to do them.

Before it could all get too embarrassing, the PE teacher from the playground arrived, and, to my delight, turned out to speak much better English than anyone else. He was keen to learn more commands to use on his marching groups, and I obliged by telling him "quick march!" "hop!," and "star jump!" by way of a belated and petty revenge on those children who had refused to answer my questions in the classroom.

At last, I was taken to meet the headmaster, where, I knew, I would finally have to say that I really didn't want to teach there at all. After a brief introduction, we went in convoy to a restaurant in town where the negotiations were to take place. Five of us sat around one side of a large round table. Each of us had a pot of boiling stock in front of us, in which a fearsome array of food was cooked. The others tucked hungrily in whilst I felt awkward and scoured the table for something I could identify.

Presently, the headmaster looked up from his food and squawked something at Mr Guo. Mr Guo then promptly filled up my tumbler with a clear liquid that came from a suspicious-looking bottle. He called it baijiu.

"You must drink with him!" he ordered, and I, keen to find anything that might take the edge off my awkwardness, meekly agreed, although it was barely eleven o'clock in the morning. Following Mr Guo's instructions, I raised my glass, shouted "ganbei!" and emptied it down my throat. It was syrupy and foul tasting. It was also very strong – over 60 % ABV. I had to control myself to hold back the retching. I should have tried my best to smile and resolved never to touch the filthy drink again. But the teachers cheered in a good-natured way, and I felt less of an outsider for a moment. So, like an adolescent being corrupted for the first time, I foolishly accepted another glass. And another. After three of these I would have happily agreed to teach English to a pride of hungry lions, and clearly spotting this, they opened negotiations.

They suggested that I teach ten hours a week, for a salary of four hundred kuai a month – about £25. Somewhere through the baijiu mist, I remembered thinking that that was a lot of work for very little money. But I was in good spirits, and didn't want to ruin such a good meal with a vulgar discussion over money, so I began to happily nod away, agreeing to every ludicrous demand they had.

I was almost beyond the point of no return, when Mr Guo made his fatal mistake. One of the other teachers had been saying something about money, when he suddenly stopped, glanced at me and blushed. Mr Guo looked over to me, and then back to the teacher. "Don't worry about him!" he said, "he can't understand anything!" It was in fact the only thing that I had understood of the whole discussion, and it riled. With a start I woke up to what I was agreeing to. The fog in my brain lifted for a moment, a shot of adrenaline jolted me, and I realised how nearly I had fallen for their simple plan of getting me drunk.

And this, after I had spent a whole evening and most of the morning steeling myself to say no. I felt ashamed of myself, and angry with everyone else. I became blunt and stubborn, suddenly refusing to do any teaching at all.

"I never wanted to teach, and I never want to teach" I petulantly repeated again and again as Mr Guo tried to work out what had caused this volte-face. They were all confused, and then unfriendly. Soon after, the party broke up, and after the most perfunctory "good-byes," I was left to get a taxi back to the dormitory on my own. I have never seen good grace evaporate so quickly, but I would rather offend them than have been forced to teach, and I felt ever so slightly smug as I settled drunkenly down to my studies that evening.

Learning Chinese is a painful experience, at least to begin with. I hadn't yet started my lessons, but I had bought my books, and I sat at my desk for hours on that second evening, faithfully copying out characters in preparation for my first lesson the next day. Over the hours, my smugness was gradually replaced with frustration. I tried in vain to make my characters look like single entities, and not just meaningless groups of squiggles. As I copied, I tried to force my brain to see meaning in the shapes I drew. Gradually, so gradually, I began to link together the smatterings of ink with the pinyin ('pinyin' is the standard system used to write Chinese words in roman letters) word, to link the pinyin with the sound, and finally to link everything to the meaning of the word. In half an hour, I managed to bind up four characters into these little bundles of knowledge. Soon though, my mind wandered off, trying to calculate how long, at this rate, it would take to learn the 2500 characters that they say that you need to know in order to read a Chinese newspaper. When it all got too much, I pretended that I was hungry as an excuse for a break, and wandered down to the kitchen. By the time I got back with my pot noodles in hand, whatever it was that had held the neat packages of knowledge together had disintegrated, and all I was left with were the blots of ink and unfamiliar sounds bouncing around my head.

Chapter 3

I was rather excited by the prospect of meeting Jim and Heather. They were an American couple who were teaching at the University and whose homepage I had found when I was trying to find out about Qiqihaer on the Internet. It was they who had told me how I should apply to the University. In an odd sort of way, I had come to view them as a celebrity couple: I had read all about their exploits on their internet blog, but I had never met them. I knew all about their 'public' image, but I had no idea what they would really turn out to be like. Also, I had not spoken English to a fellow native speaker for three days, and I was in desperate need of a fluent conversation.

I first met Heather in the entrance hall of the dormitory. She was on her way back from teaching, and wore black fur earmuffs on her head, and a long coat that looked as if it had been made from a sleeping bag. Lu, our guard, was kneeling on the floor, cutting out letters to put on a banner. Heather didn't see me at first, and wandered over to look at what the banner was going to say.

"Qiqihaer University wilcumes (sic) the department foreign Chinese teaching from The Napier University United Kingdom into China's power crane city" she read, and burst into giggles. "Does anyone know what "Napier University is?" she turned over to where I was standing.

"It is in Edinburgh, but what is all that about 'China's power crane city'?"

“Oh, that is the birds. There is a nature reserve with loads of cranes just outside the city. They are inordinately proud of it. Are you English?” she was clearly surprised.

“Yes, I’m Ben. I emailed you last year.”

“Ohhhh,” she said, delving back in her memory, “I remember. So, you came?” she paused. “Why?” Almost everyone that I had spoken to before I had gone to Qiqihaer had asked me that; I was to discover that almost everyone that I met after I arrived there was equally bemused. I mumbled something about the purity of the Mandarin accent, and changed the subject. We chatted for a few minutes, before Heather left to find some lunch. She seemed funny, and normal, and I was immensely relieved to have met her.

Later that day I met Jim. He was working away in the kitchen when I wandered in to make a cup of tea during a contrived break in my own studies. He looked ever so slightly Asian, and I was confused for a moment; he didn’t look anything like the burly America builder that I had, for some reason, imagined. I thought for a moment that he was one of the Koreans who lived in the building, and I waved and said “Ni Hao” in an unsure voice.

“Hey!” he replied, “you must be Ben!” I felt rather foolish for my mistaking him for a Korean, but he quickly put me at ease. He explained that his mother was Korean.

Jim and I chatted for a while, and he gave me a few tips on where to buy coffee, where to eat, and also told me about the other foreigners in town: there were two other Americans, George, a Professor of modern American literature who was teaching, and Judy, a retired US Navy medic who was studying Chinese. There were also five Austrians – Manfred, Joseph, Stefan, Lukas and Theo – who were teaching spoken English at the university as an alternative to doing military service back home. These nine, with some comings and goings, and along with a Russian called Dawei and some Buriat

Russian girls (the Buriats come from around lake Baikal, look very Asian, and are fiercely proud of being *Buriat*, and not Russian) were to make up my English speaking circle in Qiqihaer.

Chapter 4

The year before I went to Qiqihaer, I had worked in Shanghai for a few months. When I had been arranging my job there, I had exchanged emails with a person named Linda Ji. Over the course of twenty or so emails, I had built up a friendly relationship with Linda, and I looked forward to having a friendly face in the office when I first arrived. Imagine my surprise when I finally arrived at the office, and a sixteen stone oaf of a man wobbled up to me and announced, "I write email to you!"

"What?" I thought, "Who is this lunatic?" and began looking around wildly for an escape route. Seeing my confusion, he looked a little put out, but continued insistently.

"I write to you, you write to me: I am Linda Ji!" It was my first experience of the phenomenon of Chinese peoples' English names. They choose names that sound good to them, unaware of the meanings that these names may have in English. When I was in Shanghai, I used to have a fascination with finding out as many of these absurdities as I could. I heard of a girl called 'Kinky Ho,' I met a girl called 'Miao Miao' ("like the noise a cat makes," she explained) and I even heard a rumour of a man called 'Shitty Wang' – apparently he thought that the use of a swear word would make him sound 'edgy' and 'cool.' Later, in Qiqihaer, Stefan told me about one of his students who had chosen the name 'Hitler' – worryingly, after his hero. For the four months that I was in Shanghai, I laughed heartily at these and many hundreds of other amusing names. In Shanghai, thc Chinese were too polite to laugh at *my* name. In Qiqihaer, I was not let off so lightly.

"Ben," I would say, holding out my hand.

“Ben,” they would repeat, ignoring my hand, “Ben, Ben, Ben” they went on, saying it in different tones, and playing around with the sound. Suddenly it would hit them, “Ben!” they would shout, and squeal with laughter. “Ben, Ben, Ben!” they would continue in rising delight. I would stand there, my outstretched hand starting to droop, and my face starting to redden. I had been through this painful process several times before Joseph finally explained the problem to me.

“They say ‘Ben’ with precisely the tone that means ‘stupid.’ They are calling you ‘stupid.’ ” So I started calling myself Benjamin, and stopped laughing at their choices of English names.

Chapter 5

After just a week, I was feeling well settled. I woke early, partly because light was streaming through the window, partly so that I could finish my homework for the day, and partly because the hot water was turned on for half an hour between 6.30 and 7 am, and made a sucking, gurgling noise that it was impossible to sleep through. I always got out of bed just as the hot water finished, and had to get used to gaspingly cold showers.

Manfred introduced me to a dingy little restaurant for breakfast that served doughy balls filled with minced pork called baozi. I loved soaking them in delicious Chinese vinegar and ate huge platefuls. I became such a regular customer that soon I no longer needed to order; they knew what I would want without my having to ask.

Normally my lessons started at eight, and ran until midday. I was the only student in my class, which meant that I got full attention. It also meant that the University was really rather irritated at having to give put on classes purely for my benefit. I had four different teachers, and they fitted me in as and when they could, so sometimes my lessons would end up being in the afternoon. On Mondays and Tuesdays I was taught by a heavily made up middle aged woman who's name I never really got the hang of, so I just called Teacher. She spoke not a word of English, and so tried heroically to illustrate grammatical points using hand gestures and encouraging nods alone, but who would not tolerate even the slightest deviation from the correct pronunciation. On Wednesdays I had Teacher Lisa, a sour faced middle aged woman with short hair and shorter patience. On Thursdays I had a plump and jovial teacher called Soong, and on Fridays I was taught by Teacher Zhang. She was the most senior teacher, and the only one who spoke English.

Because of this, she was landed with the unenviable task of trying to untangle the web of confusions and misunderstandings that had grown up in my mind over the previous four days of bungled gesticulated explanations.

The pace of learning was at once onerously fast, and painfully slow. I studied all day, but still I couldn't even hold a basic conversation in Chinese. It was frustrating, and made worse by the fact that I showed little aptitude for the language, and the textbook that I was using seemed to be deliberately complicating matters.

"Unaspirated voiceless frontal-alveolar affricate. First the front part of the tongue is spread and is pressed against the upper alveolar ridge, then the tongue-tip moves apart to let out the air stream through the narrow passage." So my textbook began describing the sound that should be made in response to the letter "Z." "The vocal chords do not vibrate," it added in a stern tone. Could anyone, ever, have successfully worked out what noise they are supposed to produce through reading this senseless gibberish? And as though that weren't enough, the process of producing the correct sound was made no easier by my teacher's efforts; I spent almost all of one Tuesday morning embroiled in a fight with my whole vocal system to try to produce the sound for 'tea' correctly. When Teacher first asked me to say the word for 'tea,' I felt the glow of smugness of one who is – at last – being asked a question to which he knows the answer.

"Cha," I said with happy confidence.

"Bu hao, bu hao" (not good, not good), scolded Teacher, "cha, bu (not) 'cha.'" And they really did sound exactly the same to me. In a hopeful search for guidance I turned to the textbook:

"Aspirated voiceless post-alveolar…"

"Oh piss off." I thought. I tried a few more utterances, all pretty much identical to my ear, but presently Teacher leaped with excitement and nodded her head frantically, indicating that I had got it right.

"Cha" I tentatively offered again, nervous lest I had lost the magic touch. Which, of course, I had. I tried it again, and again. For every ten times I said that damn word, seven resulted in a shameful shaking of the head, and three in a broad smile and exclamations of "hao, hao!" and still I was none the wiser about what I was doing wrong, or right. After the first half hour or so, Teacher decided to take a different tack, and started demonstrating with her hand, holding it out and alternately cupping and uncupping it, and chanting "cha, cha, cha," in an elaborately over-annunciated way. I made the leap of logic and realised that her hand was supposed to represent my tongue, but if this was indeed the case, then I seemed to lack the gene that allowed my tongue to perform the gymnastics that this simple word required.

"Cha, cha, cha," I dutifully repeated, wondering which of these pronunciations corresponded to the meat kebabs I had been served on my first day. I was still doing it wrong, but the determined Teacher was not going to give up on me, and now started to point at various parts of her throat as if that would give me a clue. "At least she hasn't started criticising my tones yet," I foolishly thought to myself, but no sooner has this fate-tempting thought formed than she started to do just that. This was the most irritating part of learning Chinese for me. I fully accepted that I was doing it wrong, and that it sounds ridiculous to them. But what gets me is not that, it was their total non-understanding of my difficulty:

"The tone for "cha" goes up" she said (in Chinese, but I could tell from her gesticulations what she meant), "not down then up."

"As though I hadn't bloody noticed," I fumed. "I can tell that it goes up by the horrid little line above the letters that points upwards."

But of course she understood nothing, and just looked mildly concerned at my bulging eyes and reddened complexion as anger and frustration engulfed me. She always seemed to think that it was a matter of me foolishly forgetting what tone I was supposed to do. But that was the easy part. The hard part was getting my ceaselessly disobedient voice to do the tone that I told it to, particularly when the word came in the middle of a sentence. For weeks, the only thing that I could ever get to mirror the correct tones was my head, which dutifully bobbed up and down as each word went by, giving me the appearance of a nodding dog on a lorry driver's dash board.

The worst thing about it for me was that it was not a problem that I could ignore and would just go away. I really *had* to get it right, impossible though that seemed at the time. And getting angry about it was utterly pointless. It spawned a feeling of total helplessness and inadequacy that I had not felt since a moment of wanton over confidence in my abilities had led to me finding myself sat in the Oxford entrance Maths exam. But that torture only lasted for three hours, and afterwards I could go home, forget about any mathematical ambitions I may have had, and console myself with that traditional last comfort for my failures: that I didn't really want to succeed anyway. But this time I didn't have that comfort; I knew that I really did want to succeed in at least reaching a reasonable level of Chinese. I wanted be able to talk to the people that I met in the streets, to make friends, and to try to understand their unique country. At the time, that seemed an impossible dream.

Chapter 6

On the Monday of my second week, it was 'women's day,' and the Buriat girls and the Austrians had organised a party and asked me to come along. I didn't really know any of them before that evening, but I was lonely so I appreciated the invitation.

The Buriat girls cooked a myriad of Russian dishes: dumplings and various other stodge. Then Manfred (over-) cooked a fillet of beef which was then allowed to go stone cold, while we waited for the other Russian girls to get dolled up, and was finally served with an admirably experimental sauce. I have always been a fan of experimental cooking, but rarely have I met someone else so pleased to play this game as Manfred. I am used to my slightly eccentric culinary ideas being met with howls of derisive laughter and quickly forgotten. But no sooner had I suggested to Manfred that he put some strawberry jam in with the red wine sauce, than he had not only poured in half the pot, but also had reached for the Nesquick and chucked most of that in as well. For reasons that I can't quite remember, we decided against adding coffee, and perhaps for that reason, the sauce ended up being disgusting. But we had fun making it, and for the first time I felt that I wasn't totally alone.

We ate the meal in the Austrians' kitchen, and after dinner we moved the table away to make a dance floor. We had a small CD player, and later on Lukas and Dawei played some almost recognisable songs on their guitars.

I sat next to Dawei at dinner, and tried hard to hold a meaningful conversation with him. He was from Sayanogorsk, which stands on the bank of the Enisei river in the heart of Siberia. He spoke excellent Chinese, but little English.

“They do this,” he said, putting a plastic bag over his head and leaving me totally certain that I had lost the thread of his narrative. “And,” he continued, now whipping the bag off again and grabbing a bowl from the table “this full of water. One year, there none left.” He looked at me expectantly and I realised that I was expected to comment.

“Oh yes,” I ventured “quite.”

“One year, it gone, it has…” he continued, kindly ignoring my confusion.

“Evaporated!” It was like the feeling of getting a crossword clue when you are sure that it is the right answer, but just have no idea why. What could these people of whom Dawei spoke possibly be doing with plastic bags and evaporating substance? Suddenly, as I put it together like that, it struck me; he was talking about people glue sniffing. Now I only had to figure out why.

Conversations with Dawei tended to follow this pattern. But in that sort of society where you have few people to draw your circle of friends from, you learn to overlook such petty things as not being able to communicate properly. He was an exceptionally kind man, he helped me in innumerable ways when I first arrived in Qiqihaer, and soon we became good friends.

Later on in the evening I spoke at length to Manfred. He had spent a year in Glasgow and spoke with a strange Austrian / Scottish accent. He had been in Qiqihaer for a year, and was due to leave in two months time. He told me about the place, and I listened intently, lapping up every detail.

I remember being shocked by a story of one of his Chinese friends who had started at the University the year before. She had been given a form to fill in asking her for her criticism of the university. These she duly listed, and was promptly called in by the head teacher who informed her that if she continued to put negative comments down when asked for her criticisms, then she would find herself in a great deal of trouble. This was a classic technique employed by Chairman Mao in the 'hundred flowers' campaign: he asked everyone to express their opinions about how he was governing the country, and then weeded out anyone who is foolish enough to think that he was doing anything other than a perfect job. The idea that this still went on, and in my own University, made the dark history of Chinese Communism that in Shanghai had seemed so much in the past, seem suddenly very close at hand.

He also fascinated me with tales of the local customs. Groups of old men collect together in clubs, and swim together every day of the year in the Nenjiang River that flows around the city. In the summer they can relax on the sandy shore of the river, and there are lines of brightly painted wooden beach huts for them to get changed in. There are stalls selling ice creams, and the whole scene is rather idyllic. For the winter months however, the river is frozen solid. Not to be deterred, these plucky old men head out with axes and spades, and dig pits in to ice until they get through to the unfrozen water two or three metres down. They then whip off all of their clothes, and jump in.

"I think we should join them his weekend," said Manfred, ludicrously.

"Definitely," I heard myself saying, and spent the week praying that he would forget by the weekend.

I must have made an alright impression at that first party, because on Friday night at nine thirty in the evening, just as I was shutting down my computer and starting to think of jumping into my pyjamas, Manfred knocked on my door and asked me if I wanted to "go and have a quick beer" with the Guang Fong (the shopkeeper from over the road) and his wife. I do love my early nights, but I had been all week at my desk, and I was once again craving social interaction. So I agreed to go.

It soon transpired that since there really were no bars to speak of in the city, the venue for our "quick beer" was to be a nearby restaurant. And while we were there, it seemed churlish not to tuck into just a little food. So the nine of us tucked in to an enormous second dinner that went on for just over three hours. I think that I probably ate and drank more than most, excesses that I more than balanced out by being totally deficient in the conversation department. Because the idea was that the Austrians wanted to take the shopkeeper and his wife out for a drink, that had now turned in to dinner, all the conversation was with them, and in Chinese, scuppering my chances of understanding anything. I could by then understand just a few words, and could try to guess at what the general line of conversation was. But every ten minutes or so, Joseph made a strange gurgling noise, half way between a sigh and a cough, which meant that he was ready to give me a bite sized summary of events; this always showed me to have totally missed the point.

As I sat drinking and eating in my own little bubble, the snippets that were translated for me often set me off on a long internal discussion, quite detached from everyone else present. For example, Guang Fong quoted a local saying that if you go to drink with a Dongbei (Manchurian) man, you must take two bottles of baijiu for him: you put one on the table for him to drink at once, and you put one underneath, so that he can continue drinking once he has lost the ability to sit on his chair. I laughed, but it was not the first time that I had heard grown men in Qiqihaer keenly boasting in a, frankly, rather childish way about their supposed prowess in matters of alcohol, and for me it rankled slightly. It made it hard not to view them in a slightly patronising way.

Another little tit-bit fuelled this fledgling anti-Chinese train of thought, and turned it into a full-scale internal rant. It was a riddle that had been set by Guang Fong's daughter. It goes like this: there are three pigs in a line, the one at the front says "there are two pigs behind me" then the next one says "there is one pig behind me, and one pig in front of me" finally, the third pig says "there are two pigs behind me." How is this possible? I had the (wrong) answer in a flash: the third pig was walking backwards. I was being too pragmatic. This is China, and so the correct answer is that the third pig is lying. Funny though this may be, the thought that a seven year old child has enough cynicism to concoct that kind of riddle just made my heart bleed. I don't know if that can honestly be used as solid evidence of the endemic nature of lying in this country, but I used it nonetheless, and started mulling over to myself just how awful the Chinese were.

Mr Guo had started off my general distrust of what Chinese people said to me, with his constant stream of lies and deceptions. Until now, I had limited myself to viewing him as a compulsive liar. Now I started to think to myself that this was a more widespread problem. In a weak effort at backing up this wild blanket insult, I seized on my experience buying a DVD player. I had decided on the one I wanted: a nice brand new one, with a picture of a lively blue cat prancing about on the box that inspired my confidence. We went off for a few minutes to look for a TV to link up with this player, and then returned to pick it up. Dawei started, rather rudely, I thought, to ask if them if they had switched the DVD player in the box over with a second hand one. "No, no, no!" cried the shopkeeper, looking (as I felt he had the right to) rather offended. Much to my surprise, Dawei's suspicions were not sated by this honest assurance, and he insisted on opening the box up to reveal…. A second hand DVD player. The shopkeeper smiled in an amused way, and cheerfully switched the players back, seemingly totally unembarrassed by being rumbled in his criminal scam. As I thought over this story again, I suddenly had a change of heart and tried to view this (to my eyes) unattractive trait in an unbiased light; there must, I thought, just be some different way of viewing it. Maybe everyone is expected just to lie, and that is that. I have certainly noticed a less criminal form of lying when people here just want to tell you what they think that you want to hear. For example, one of Mr Guo's more minor deceptions was when I asked him if there was hot water all day. "Yes," he said, thinking that that was what I wanted to hear, and unaware of the fact that I would rather have the truth told to me directly than find it out abruptly for myself as I shivered in the icy shower. But still, even in the most liberal moment of my internal discussions that evening, I couldn't see how you could build a society where people are so reluctant to tell the truth.

Just as this private anti-Chinese rant was drawing to its disapproving conclusion, I heard Joseph making that noise again, and turned to see what had happened. Manfred had got up to try to subtly pay the bill before the Chinese had a chance to offer, thus avoiding the painful scene of arguing over who pays, only to find out that Guang Fong and his wife (who, I might add, lived on a shelf in the shop, just above the stationary aisle) had paid for the whole thing as soon they had arrived. Such generosity quite took the wind out of my rant's sails, and the feeling of what a wonderful race they are came flooding back. I often found that my opinions would fluctuate like this. I suppose it comes of living in such an unfamiliar world.

As Manfred bade me goodnight he said, "What time shall we go to the swimming tomorrow," and my heart sank.

"Ten o'clock" I muttered, and went to bed for a sleepless night.

Chapter 7

At ten o'clock the next morning, I slunk down stairs to find that our little expedition had attracted rather more support than I wanted: Manfred and Dawei were both keen to swim, and a gaggle of Chinese, Americans and Austrians were keen to watch and laugh.

As we walked, I tried to find a legitimate reason for not joining in.

"Is the river very polluted?" I asked hopefully.

"No – Mr Guo says that it is one of only four unpolluted rivers in China" George replied, and laughed. I think he knew that I was trying to wriggle out of my drunken commitment, and I think that he also knew quite how little respect I had for Mr Guo's claims. But still, that line of argument was clearly not going to wash.

The river itself was desolately beautiful. It was a huge swathe of white sweeping between the edge of the city and the barren brown land on farther shore. We stumbled down the flood protection wall, and onto the frozen sand of the shoreline. It was a relatively warm day, and the ice was melting in places in the sun. As we reached the river itself, I could see that the ice on top had become slushy, and there were puddles in places.

"It looks a bit dangerous" I tried tentatively, but everyone laughed and pointed to a mule dragging a heavily loaded cart out near the middle. It looked as if I really was going to have to join in.

We found a group of the mad old men in the process of digging another pool. About forty of them were huddled around a small hole in the ice, watching while three men busted their backs smashing enormous hammers again and again against the frozen river. Someone told them what we wanted to do, and they howled with excited laughter. After much chattering, a group of them led us off to the far bank.

Traversing the river was an unsettling twenty minute walk, which I spent trying desperately to ignore the yawning chasm of blackness beneath my feet. I knew that it must be safe, but it was an eerie experience, and my nerves were feeling fragile.

We arrived to find that the 'pool' was situated where a tributary joined the main river. The river was shallow here, and the ice was thin. The old men had managed to smash out a pool that stretched for about thirty metres, and was about five metres wide. When I got there, they were standing in a huddle by the edge, pointing at the ice and discussing something with Manfred.

"Any problems?" I asked, but he answered with a confident "No," so I went to get changed. It was a warm day by local standards, but it couldn't have been much above –15 Celsius. This is not a temperature to be running around in nothing but swimming trunks. I held all my clothes in a bundle around my body, and rushed around in circles, trying to keep, if not warm, then at least alive. After a minute of this, Dawei ambled over to me.

"I think is more easier if we swim," he pointed out, after I had slipped over for the third time. I dusted the snow off my arm and admitted that maybe he was right: "If it were done when 'tis done, then 'twere well it were done quickly."
It was not cold in any normal sense of the word. I struggle to remember exactly, but I recall something in my neurobiology studies about 'cold' receptors, and how they only work within specific temperature boundaries. I am pretty certain that this was outside those boundaries. It didn't feel *cold*. It felt like death. My lungs froze, my head writhed from the pain of a headache like the ones that too much ice cream can give you – only worse. I flailed

my limbs wildly to try to keep them working as I quickly lost feeling, and I think that I probably screamed quite a lot as well. It was not a dignified sight.

After what seemed like minutes, but in reality was probably about 5 seconds, I thrashed towards the edge, and tried to wrench myself out with my numbed arms. An evil old man placed his hand on my head, and shoved me back in, laughing heartily. At the time, I didn't even feel truly angry with him; that was a luxury that I could not afford myself. I was thinking only of survival. I plunged back into the pool, and my head was submerged for a moment. I spluttered back to the surface and made again for the side. At last, a few seconds later, I found a more friendly section of the bank, and was hauled out to safety by Heather and Jim.

I remember very little of the next few moments, except a sudden and brief warmth followed by excruciating pain as blood returned to my extremities. Once again I ran in circles, and clutched my clothes, until – at last – the pain had receded enough for me to get dressed.

As we made to return home, laughing and slapping each others' backs in a fit of camaraderie, I turned back for a last look at the pool and witnessed a delicious example of poetic justice: there was a sharp 'Crack!' and a section of the bank crumbled into the water, taking with it the evil man who had thrust me back in when I was struggling for my life. Until then I had forgotten about him. He dragged himself onto the bank and wailed in anger and frustration and pain. I roared with laughter in a most ungentlemanly fashion, and almost skipped back home in delight.

It may not surprise you to learn that I awoke the next morning with a streaming cold. Outside the wind was howling. Normally the sound of the wind is a comforting sound to me; it makes me want to curl up in front of a fire with a thick blanket and good book. In Scotland I have happily sat out many streaming colds in this way; a little stone highland cottage has been designed to feel cosy in exactly these weather conditions. But this time, although I had a stack of fifty or so DVDs, and a comfortable bed to help me relax, the atmosphere just wasn't quite right. The buildings there just aren't cosy. They are all built to the same stark, unfriendly plan. They have thin concrete walls that keep the worst of the wind off, but the seal on the windows has always long since disappeared, and an icy draught constantly finds its way into the room. The plastic sheet stuck on the inside of the window did help to stop the draught coming into the room, but it rustled constantly, meaning that you could never forget that there was a problem. And all of the rooms are about nine feet tall, meaning that any warmth that is produced by the barely functioning heating system floats in a useless blanket about a foot above your head if you are standing up. It doesn't make snuggling up in front of the TV a very appealing idea.

But I had no other option, so I wrapped myself up in my scratchy duvet, switched on a DVD, and started wondering to myself – in a self pitying way – if anyone would notice that I was ill.

Lunchtime came and went, and I moved on to my second DVD. I kept trying to remember if you are supposed to 'feed a fever, starve a cold' or the other way around. Either way, it wasn't important; I couldn't muster the energy to go and grapple with a restaurant at the moment, so I would just have to starve my cold.

At about six, Jim knocked on my door to see if I wanted to go for some supper. My self-pitying side was a little annoyed at the fact that someone had already come to see me; I really had no cause to feel all the oppressive loneliness in which I had been wallowing. And what is more, on hearing that I was ill, Jim offered to pick me up a takeaway at the restaurant. He and Heather did the same for me for every meal the next day.

As though this wasn't enough, Dawei heard about my illness, and became convinced that it was because I had been walking around my room in bare feet; he said that the tiled floor was too cold and had made me ill. So on the second day he appeared with a large amount of the most hideously brightly coloured spongy matting, which fitted together like a jigsaw puzzle and would stop my feet from having to touch the floor. I can't say that I necessarily agree with his medical reasoning, but all in all, I couldn't really have asked for more concern or kindness if I had been at home in the bosom of my family.

After two days of takeaway food, my room was starting to smell of stale soy sauce and I decided that the time had come to empty my bin. I had heard rumours of there being a bin-emptying point somewhere at the other end of the corridor. So I intrepidly set off, bin in hand, to have a look about. I tried a couple of likely looking doors, but found them locked. I was on the point of giving up when a kindly Korean appeared, guessed what I was after (not a huge leap of imagination needed, seeing as I was brandishing a bin, but I had learned to be impressed by anyone who showed the slightest understanding of my intentions), and decided to help me out. She took me to a little door in the end wall of the building; a little square thing rather like those night-safes outside banks, and opened it up to reveal a small garbage shoot. I have always rather wanted to see one of these things in action and so was pleasantly surprised to find one here, in my very own building.

I had already started to tip the bin forward to pour in my offering when the Korean snapped the door shut saying, "but this too narrow, so," she continued, flinging open the nearby window, "we put here," pointing outside. I leaned tentatively and slightly sceptically out of the window, and looked down four floors to where an enormous heap of rubbish was busy climbing its' way up the North wall of the building. It seems that when your bin fills up, you just throw the contents out of the window.

I wrestled for a moment with the dark feeling, a result no doubt of an upbringing filled with strict rules about litter, that there was something very wrong in all of this, before throwing caution and, strangely enough, three pot noodle pots, two cans of coke, the skin of a few tangerines and countless other scraps of rubbish, to the wind. A sudden gust caught one of the pot noodle pots and took it far to the west of the main pile. Now you may call me "litter bug!" if you wish, but as I watched that little red plastic pot dancing on the wind, adding itself to the city-wide rubbish tip that is Qiqihaer, I felt that rush of excitement that naughtiness sometimes invokes; it was like the never-to-be-as-good-again excitement of that first cigarette in the bushes at school. Soon, like smoking, I would get used to this routine and it would lose its allure, and luckily, unlike smoking, it was not actually addictive. But for the first few weeks I always looked forward to my bin filling up again so that I could hurl the contents out of the window.

Chapter 8

By the beginning of my third week in Qiqihaer, I was starting to feel quite well settled. I had the makings of a circle of friends, and I no longer felt as isolated and lonely as I had when I first arrived. But with this greater stability came a waning in the excitement I felt for the city: when I had first arrived, it had been an enormous – and slightly intimidating – mystery. Now that I had found some sort of a place in it, it no longer seemed so overbearing, and had consequently lost some of its allure. In hindsight this seems peculiarly contrary of me, but that was how I felt.

I think that this disillusionment with the city had come partly as a result of growing familiarity, and partly as a result of my difficulties in learning the language. I had envisaged afternoons spent wandering and exploring the city, chatting to people that I met in the streets. It was now obvious that this fantasy would not come true for an extremely long time.

In spite of many assurances from Mr Guo, I was still only receiving ten hours of lessons each week, instead of the twenty that I had paid for. It was becoming clear that I would never be given the full quota.

I had become settled in a routine, and this routine did not involve speaking very much Chinese. Other than occasional trips to the shop and the restaurant, I really had very little interaction with Chinese people. The people that I met in both of these places knew full well that I couldn't speak Chinese and so, although they were very friendly, they didn't really talk to me much. The only Chinese people who really tried to make conversation with me on a regular basis were those seeking a "language partner." This was an aspect of life in a city with very few native English speakers that I had not foreseen: you are seen as a precious commodity. Anyone who is ambitious in China needs to speak English. And to get good at English you need to find a native speaker to practice with. So every time you leave the foreigners dormitory, you are pounced on by hoards of people wanting to become your "language partner." They claim that they will teach you Chinese as you teach them English, but it is clear who will get the best of the bargain. The incompetence with which they try to persuade you is fascinating:

"I am Chinese," they would often superfluously begin, "I want to make friends with a foreigner to improve my English. Will you be my friend?" It is hardly the most flattering of introductions. Wherever I went I was followed by these ambitiously smiling faces, dead set on pinning me down.

But in the midst of this dissatisfaction, I saw the potential for great things. I saw that if I arranged for my meagre ten hours of lessons to be bunched up into the middle of the week, it would leave me with four day weekends. I could then use these long weekends to travel around Heilongjiang, meeting people and 'discovering' (there was that pretentious imagination at work again) the ways of rural China. Heilongjiang is not famous for having beautiful scenery. I could not realistically expect to see things that would rival even High Wycombe in terms of pure, unspoiled natural beauty. But because of this lack of beauty, no guide book had paid even the slightest attention to this area the size of England. The very fact that I would be discovering these places for myself, without the *Lonely Planet* to tell me exactly what to expect and where to get good Western food, could, I hoped, render even the most uninteresting places exciting. I bought myself a map of the area and started plotting.

I had never yet travelled alone in China, and although pawing over the incomprehensible characters – there was no English language map available – written in the remoter parts of the map gave me a rush of excitement, I knew that my first adventure would have to be a little closer to home. I had long harboured a genuine interest in the provincial capital, Harbin, and decided to go there that weekend. Harbin is three hours southwest of Qiqihaer, and was once a centre of great importance known to some as 'little Moscow.' It was ceded to the Russians in the late 19th century, when it was no more than a tiny fishing village, as a station for the China Eastern railway. It had grown into a prosperous and – apparently – beautiful city, and still retained much of the Russian architecture to this day. It is a larger city than Qiqihaer, and there are many more foreigners living there, so it was not an especially adventurous choice, but my travels had to start somewhere.

Having made this decision, I felt much more comfortable about settling down to the week's routine. But on top of my lessons, I felt that I should try to see a bit of whatever 'culture' Qiqihaer had to offer, before I set off to explore new towns. So it was that on Wednesday afternoon Stefan, Dawei and I set off to find the Qiqihaer museum.

It was a large and almost grand building that had recently been put up not far from the north gate of the University. It was a surprising mix of neo-palladian and Chinese styles, rendered in the ubiquitous concrete. It wasn't really beautiful, but it was at least quite impressive and held promise of a reasonable museum inside. Above the doorway were written the characters for 'museum,' but although I had been studying them that morning, I was unable to recognise the stylised way that they were written. As Dawei read them out I felt a pang of annoyance and grief at my stupidity.

At the entrance we argued for a few minutes with a woman who didn't seem to believe that we actually wanted to go inside. Eventually she reluctantly took five kuai off each of us, and dragged the door open in a disconsolate way as though to say "I *tried* to warn you…"

The first room contained about eight life-sized replicas of terracotta warriors. These were very poorly and unconvincingly done. They had been smattered in brown paint to try to make them look old, but in fact it only made them look new but dirty. Behind these there were some smaller models of two horse drawn carriages, also from the terracotta army. These were even worse: not only were they really quite small, but they were very badly made. The faces were blank, and the carts had huge splodges of glue dripping from every joint. Finally, in the corner there were some tiny models of terracotta soldiers – no more then six inches tall – standing in a glass case.

We walked quickly around the room, laughing at the absurdity of filling a museum with models of artefacts found at a site about a thousand miles away. It didn't hold our amusement for long however, and after a minute or so we were searching for the next room. We circled the room three or four times, sure that we must have missed some small opening, until we swallowed our pride and decided to ask the guard. The conversation was in Chinese, but I could understand well enough what was said.

"Where is the rest of the museum?"

"Eh?"

"The rest of the museum?" pause. "I mean, this can't be all of it… can it?" We all looked furtively around at the pathetic collection of replicas.

"Yes." And it was. The whole of the Qiqihaer museum consisted of a handful of badly sculpted clay models. To add further insult, as we left the room we noticed a small stall set up in the lobby selling the six inch tall terracotta warriors for just ten kuai each. It seemed rather cheeky to charge us five kuai to look at some models in a glass box, and then to ask for another ten in order to buy them.

The woman who had let us in looked at us with an ill-concealed 'I told you so!' expression on her face, and we couldn't help laughing. She muttered something incomprehensible, and the other two reacted with nods and smiles.

Stefan turned to me, "She says that because we are the first foreign visitors, we can see the special exhibition that is on at the moment for free."

"What is the special exhibition?" I asked sceptically.

"Something about Mao. I didn't really understand." We all expected that it would be an entertaining propaganda exhibition glorifying the life of the 'great helmsman.' If I had not had two proficient Chinese readers with me, I might have left with the impression that it had been this sort of exhibition, and that I had missed something of mild interest.

But that was not the case. Stefan and Dawei translated the captions with growing hilarity and disbelief. It turned out that it was mainly an exhibition of photographs of people going to see exhibitions glorifying the life of the 'great helmsman' in other parts of China: not famous people, just people. Peasants were seen queuing up in everywhere from Yunan to Hunan, from Kashgar to Qingdao , all mustard keen, or so the captions would have us believe, to find out how wonderful Mao had been. It was quite extraordinary. There were other photographs that showed items loosely associated with Mao. My favourite was one that showed a hoe that had been found in Mao's village and so might have been seen or even used by him, but probably hadn't.

As we left, shaking our heads in disbelief and chuckling to ourselves, the guard came over to us and, obviously slightly embarrassed by the standard of the museum that we had been subjected to, suggested that we went to another museum around the corner. We had no other plans for the afternoon – this museum had only taken up about fifteen minutes of the two hours that we had expected – and so we pressed on in search of cultural fulfilment.

This next museum was built on the sight of the Qing dynasty government house. The guides claimed that these were the original buildings, but I didn't believe them. The bricks were too crisp and sharp at the edges to be more than a year or two old, and the whole place just had a very *new* feel to it. Nonetheless, it proved to be mildly interesting.

Only one of the buildings was yet open: this had been the residence of an important general. They had furnished the house as it might have been furnished when the general had lived there, I suppose it was intended to give an idea of the times. The first couple of rooms were filled with what looked to me like rather poor quality replicas of Qing dynasty furniture, but which the four curators who were showing us around claimed were all genuine antiques.

In the third room we found some samurai swords, and since no one seemed to mind, we took them out of their scabbards and play fought with them. I know nothing about swords or sword fighting, but these felt beautifully balanced, and swishing them around your head gave you a dangerous sense of power. Luckily, before anything got too out of hand, we were side tracked by an old gramophone player. The handle that powered the turntable had broken, but Dawei had found a very old record and we were able to get some sound out of the machine by turning it manually. It was some dreary piano music; not wonderful, and the record was badly scratched, but it was fun to be in a museum that let you play with everything.

I pushed them too far in the next room though, and with what I thought was an entirely innocent action. This was the general's study and, much to my surprise and delight, behind his desk in the corner of the room was an enormous plastic model of him. It was ludicrously large – his head alone was over a foot and a half tall –

and wore the most comical expression. In my delight, I pulled out my camera and took a snap of him. At this, the bonhomie of our guides evaporated. They shouted incomprehensibles that I took to be offensive, and marched us from the building. They left us, bemused and giggling, on the main road outside.

As we walked back to the dormitory, we tried to make sense of what we had seen. The offence at taking a photograph was strange, but ultimately quite understandable; it was just against the rules. What was more bizarre was the uselessness of the museums themselves. Why build a museum if you are only going to use two rooms, and you are going to fill those with rubbish? The answer, or the best that we could ever come up with, was that it was simply a 'box ticking' exercise: they had been told that to promote tourism or education or whatever, they needed to have a museum; so a museum was built. What went into it was no concern of anyone's. It was there, that was the important thing.

Chapter 9

Having thus sampled Qiqihaer's cultural delights, I set off on the train for Harbin on Friday evening.

Train stations in China are really more like airports than train stations. They have departure gates where you must wait until you train is called, and then you fight your way through the checkpoint, through a maze of corridors, and onto the train. If you are not there by ten minutes before departure time, you are unlikely to get on.

I was politely standing in the queue for one of the turn-styles waiting my turn, when from behind me I felt the aggressive shove of an elbow in the small of my back. This was no 'oooh dear, sorry, I'm just being pushed forward, sorry about this…' English-style elbow in a queue. This was the sort of elbow that sent a shot of adrenalin through my body as age-old biological systems made my body ready for 'fight or flight.' It was the sort of shove that you receive and instantly know that you will turn around to find a tattooed skin-head, his chest puffed out, his eyes wild, inquiring of you "what the fuck are you staring at?"

I tried to hide the obvious trepidation that I was feeling, and turned slowly around to find… no aggressor, but just a sea of smiling Chinese being washed this way and that under the force of their collective barging. The queue started to edge forward, and the elbowing became more frequent. With each shove, my level of anger rose; I just could not believe that you could ram your elbow into someone like that without any intention of starting a serious conflict with them. As I struggled to contain this ingrained response, I decided that the only way to understand it was to have a go myself.

So I gave the guy in front of me a little shove. He was sent flying off to the side and out of my way, and I stepped unselfconsciously (or as unselfconsciously as I could manage) forward into his place in the queue. As I passed him, I shot him a cheery glance, and was gratified to see it returned: "Good shove! No hard feelings mate!" he seemed to say. If you get stuck in with them, it is, like throwing rubbish from the window, a liberating experience to use such ostensibly aggressive behaviour in a non-aggressive way. I started to really enjoy the queue. I surged forward, a whirlwind of polite smiles and persistent elbows, then allowed myself to be overtaken, letting me repeat the process again and again. Although at times I did feel slightly like the kid in the under 11s rugby team who has beaten all his peers through puberty and so is three times the size of anyone else, it was nonetheless a lot of fun.

When we reached the 'funnel' into the turn-styles, the man in front of me was all but torn in half as he struggled to get himself the right side of the barrier, fighting the tide of the crowd. The people in the crowd behind him shouted their sympathies, and looked sorry for him. But they did not for one moment desist from pushing. They didn't seem to connect his impending doom with their shoving. It was as though they simply could not believe that any single one of them could have an effect on the force of the crowd if they just stopped pushing. So the best they could do was to shout their sympathy and keep on pushing, ripping the poor fellow to pieces.

When finally I reached the train, I sat smugly in my window seat, congratulating myself on clearing the first barrier in breaking down my Western perceptions of 'personal space,' which made being in China so stressful. Just at this moment, I felt the seat next to me vibrate and I was engulfed by that curious and vomit-inducing smell: a Chinese fart. Doubtless they feel the same of our British flatulence, but for me, the Chinese fart stands alone. And penned in as I was beside the window, I had no escape. I had to make do with wrinkling my nose in a disapproving way, and staring intently out at the expanse of nothingness that passes for the countryside around there. There were still some things I couldn't stop myself feeling.

When I arrived in Harbin, it was already dark. The square in front of the station was laced in neon, and the roads leading away at each corner were illuminated in avenues of yellow light. It felt as if I had travelled thirty years into the future after the black streets of Qiqihaer. It was late and I was tired. I couldn't face traipsing round the city in search of a good and reasonably priced hotel, so I simply made for the nearest one and hoped that it wouldn't be too expensive.

There were a small group of heavily made-up girls in the corner of the foyer, who I strongly suspected of being Russian hookers. I avoided their gaze, and strode up to the reception desk repeating the Chinese for "a single room, please" over in my head. I was always reluctant to show that I couldn't speak the language, and used to learn whatever phrase I would need from my phrasebook before I embarked on any conversation; a childish attempt at keeping 'face,' since I would invariably be unable to understand their very first reply.

I muddled through the conversation, and managed to ask how much the room would be.

"200 yuan," the receptionist replied in English.

"Oh, too expensive, too expensive!" I cried, giving up my efforts at Chinese. I haggled her down to the 'special rate' of 160 yuan, and set off towards the lift feeling quite smug. It was only the next morning when I had checked out and paid up that I noticed a huge banner that was draped across the front of the building. "All rooms 100 kuai," it boasted. I gritted my teeth and went in search of a friendlier establishment.

The main street had recently been barred to traffic and neatly cobbled in a 'city beautification' project. It had been remarkably successful. On summer evenings, the street is a throng of couples out for a gentle stroll. But on that first visit, in the tail end of the winter, it was almost empty and I was alone as I wandered along, admiring the stucco fronted buildings and peering in through frosted windows at row upon row of fur coats. It felt like a city with history, and I was happy to stroll through it for hours.

I knew that it existed, but it was quite by chance that I actually came upon the Santa Sofia Cathedral. It is a wonderful onion domed Russian orthodox Cathedral set in a large paved square surrounded on all sides by Communist China. It is rather a lovely sight. There are speakers in the top of the tower that blare out tinny musak at a great volume, firmly reminding everyone that this is no longer a place for revered worship. At the foot of the steps a mother brandished her copiously excreting child as he sprayed the stones a bright shade of yellow. Happily this soon froze, ensuring that the new colouring would be seen by every visitor until winter was finally over. I paid the inflated price for entry, and stalked my way to the front door. Inside I was immediately struck by how successful they had been in sucking all of the atmosphere out of the place. There was an exhibition of awful and very grainy photographs, and a model of the cathedral, which seemed to me to be a peculiarly pointless thing to have inside the building itself. Then there were a couple of paintings that seem to have been borrowed from a GCSE art portfolio. Finally, by the exit, a large board tried to explain the aims of the museum in broken but ambitious English. It was so littered with meaningless 'idioms,' such as "the twinklings of history shine through the light of photographical artefacts," that it was really impossible to read it and not laugh. The curator was visibly riled by my mirth, and I decided to leave before I caused any more fuss. It is an appalling waste of such a beautiful building.

In the gift shop I saw a Chinese-looking man talking to the shopkeeper in pidgin English. From this I guessed that he was

Russian. "Here! Here! Stalin!" shouted the shopkeeper pointing at a photograph that he was trying to sell, seemingly unaware that Stalin was a) not hugely popular in Russia these days, and b) that even if he were, they would surely have quite enough Stalin pictures of their own should they want them.

"I don't like Stalin," the Russian grimly replied, and moved off. I enjoyed watching this exchange as it seemed to highlight the different take the Chinese have on the nuances of world history. The Chinese respect Stalin as a 'strong leader' in the same way that they respect Hitler for being a 'strong leader.' The fact that he fell out very badly with Mao does not seem to lessen his status. But then they still love Mao, even though it is now reasonably well known, even in China, that he caused the dual disasters of the 'great leap forward' and the 'cultural revolution.' The official line is that Mao was 70% right and 30% wrong, and people seem happy to accept this. He was a 'strong leader,' and that is to be respected above all things.

Chapter 10

"Bongwuyuan," I repeated confidently, but once again received nothing but confusion from the taxi driver in return. Eventually I broke and, irritated that I had been rumbled for not speaking the language, produced my phrasebook and pointed to the translation for 'zoo.'

"Dongwuyuan!" he exclaimed, and I blushed as I realised that I was in fact guilty of just reading it wrongly. Anyway, he took me there, and I was just about to pay the substantial fare and hop out, full of excitement at the prospect of feeding chickens to tigers (for such, I had been told, was some of the entertainment to be enjoyed at Harbin zoo), when he started yabbering again. I was fairly pleased at having been able to get here without having to resort to a tiger impression. Tiger impressions, however, seemed to hold no such taboo for my driver, who now embarked on an admirable one.

"Grrr!" he growled, holding up his hands as claws, and baring his teeth.

"Grrrr!" I nodded back enthusiastically, mimicking his actions as I decided to get stuck in. He shook his head and motioned for me to get back in. We set off once again, and some forty minutes later it transpired that the zoo is not the place to see the tigers; that is the tiger park, exactly on the opposite side of the city. I suspect that he knew that this was my intended destination from the start, but after his gallant charade, I was prepared to forgive him this small extortion.

The Tiger Park was not a tasteful affair. It was decorated with rather too many papier-mâché tigers and plastic toys for my liking. My taxi driver seemed by this stage to have realised that I was something of a cash cow, and offered to wait for me. I couldn't summon up the will nor the words to tell him to leave, although I knew that he would leave the car on the meter, so I let him stay, and he performed rather a useful task in telling me where to go and what to do. I bought my ticket, and on an impulse, bought a pheasant as well. I wasn't totally sure that I was happy to pay to watch a small bird being fed to a tiger, but I consoled myself with the thought that the bird was no doubt being kept in a miserably small cage, and the tiger was also having no fun, so if I could end one lot of suffering, and alleviate another, then it wasn't such a bad thing to do. There was a further option to buy a cow for $1000. This, I felt, was a step too far. I am fond of cows, and I didn't want to see one torn limb from limb in front of me.

We set off through the stern iron gates to the tiger enclosure in a disconcertingly rickety minibus. About fifteen tigers were lolling around a brown earthy field about the size of a football pitch. We drove around in a couple of circles, coming within a few feet of some of them. When we were at our closest, the driver would beep the horn, and the Chinese tourists would bang the window to try to startle them.

We left this field, and entered another where a jeep came to meet us. The driver shouted something over to the jeep, and almost at once a mangy pheasant with clipped wings and a slightly drugged look to it was thrown out of the window. The contest of pheasant vs. 500 pound Manchurian tiger (hungry) was never going to be a close fought one. But I was hoping that the tiger may have been given a slight challenge, even if just to warm him up a bit. The moment the pheasant was thrown out of the van, the tiger started eyeing him up. The pheasant looked around in a startled manner, savouring its moment of freedom. Then the tiger made a token effort at 'slinking' towards it, before winding up into a lazy lolloping canter. In one snap the bird was dead, and the enormous beast set about plucking it. It was a strange and in some ways an awesome sight, but I didn't feel any of the excitement that was causing the Chinese tourists to whoop and shriek with delight. I certainly didn't feel inclined to go back and fork out the extra cash for a cow.

Back in our favourite local restaurant on Sunday evening I enjoyed regaling some of my new friends with tales of my adventure. I had been exploring. I had been forced to speak Chinese. And now here I was, back to tell the tale in the safety of Qiqihaer. I felt a warm glow of satisfaction when I considered the prospect of the next three months and what adventures they might hold.

In my excitement, I marked the route of this first little adventure in thick black pen on the map of Heilongjiang that I had bought. I stuck the map to my bedroom wall with some blu-tack that I had brought from home, and lay back in bed to admire it. Every morning from that day onwards, I would go to sleep and wake up looking at that map. The contorted outline of Heilongjiang – it looks a little bit like the silhouette of Dougal from 'The Magic Roundabout' – became etched in my mind and open spaces that I hadn't yet explored fuelled my dreams. Every time I left Qiqihaer, I took the map as my guidebook and every time I returned to Qiqihaer, I would stick the map once more to the wall and trace in black ink along the route that I had taken, proud and satisfied by the neat line that testified to my intrepid journey.

Chapter 11

My weekend away had highlighted just how far I had to go in learning the language. My spoken Chinese was simply terrible. Rather than feeling discouraged, however, as I had at the beginning of my third week, I was feeling excited and confident. I may not have been able to impress anyone with my Chinese at the weekend, but I had at least been understood, sometimes. That seemed to make perseverance more worthwhile.

I was also becoming fascinated by the structure of the language. Each character represents a single syllable, and a meaning. These can be built up in to words that contain more than one character, and the meanings of these words can often be worked out from the constituent characters. For example, the Chinese for 'nappy' is made up from characters that mean 'piss but don't get wet.' A little more abstractly, "immediately" is rendered in Chinese by "on a horse," presumably a leftover from the days when that was the fastest way to get something done. Other times, however, it can be very hard to work out the meaning of a word, or even that it is a word and not just two or three separate characters. Names confuse the issue still further, as here the characters are often used only phonetically, and their meaning is irrelevant. For example, 'Qiqihaer' has no meaning in Chinese. This is all very well if you know the name that you are reading, and so you know that it doesn't have any meaning. But if you are new to the game, you will spend hours looking up every character, only to discover that when taken together they have absolutely no discernable meaning.

Another way that characters can be combined is in cheng yu. 'Cheng yu' literally means 'become language.' It is more usually translated as 'proverbs,' but the use of cheng yu is far more widespread in Chinese than the use of proverbs in English, and they are a far more important linguistic device. They are always made up of four characters, and you cannot necessarily work out the meaning of the cheng yu from the constituent characters. There are normally stories behind each cheng yu that explain its meaning.

A simple example of a cheng yu is "yi lu shun feng," which means "on your way home good wind." This doesn't take a genius to work out; it is an old sailing term that has come into general use to mean "goodbye," or something similar. A more obscure one, which I prefer is "hua shi tian zu," which directly translated means "to draw a snake and add legs." The story behind it is of four men who found that they had only enough baijiu between them for one person to get good and drunk. So rather than share it out and all get just a little bit tipsy, they decided to have a competition, the winner of which would get all the booze. The competition was a simple one: the first one to draw a snake was the winner. The whistle went to signal the start of play, and all four of them set to work, furrowing their brows as they urgently sketched away. One guy, lets call him 'Wang,' was by far the speediest: he had finished up and even painted some stripes on his beast before any of the others had got beyond outlining the head. So smug was Wang at the margin of his victory that he decided to polish up his drawing still more. So he coloured in the rest of it, adding some bright green around the tail. Then he made the fangs a bit sharper and more menacing, and added some detailed scales. Finally, running out of any other realistic ideas, and still with time to waste, he drew some legs on his snake. Just because he could.

When the time came to judge the pictures, the others quite rightly objected to his beautiful creation; equipped as it was with legs, it was no longer a snake. So he lost the booze. The meaning of "to draw a snake and add legs" is to go too far, and ruin everything.

A good Chinese writer will pepper his work with these things. The more the better. The skill is to use them in exactly the right place:

you can't use "to draw a snake and add legs" in every situation that would call for "to overdo it" in English. You have to only use it in the perfect sense. For other shades of meaning that we would still use "to overdo it" for, you would have to substitute a different cheng yu. A dictionary of cheng yu has about 20,000 or so in it. These are essentially new words that must be learned on top of all everything else that you have to learn to get to grips with Chinese. I can see how it could be very gratifying; sometimes when you find a perfect situation to roll out an old cliché in English, it can be amusing. But these are different from clichés; their meaning is more oblique and you need to actually learn them before you can understand them. Because these are used often, the level of education that you have to reach to be able to appreciate even fairly low brow Chinese literature as opposed to most Western books is simply mind boggling. I suppose it is analogous to the level of musical education that you have to have in order to truly appreciate classical music as opposed to the Spice Girls.

There can be some limited logic to the way that the characters are written. The character 'hao,' meaning 'good' or 'well,' consists of a picture of a woman on the left, and the radicle meaning 'son' on the right. The idea is that a mother and son is *the* exemplar of what is 'good.' The character for 'peace' shows a woman under a roof. I am not quite sure of the implications of that, but it certainly helped me to remember how to draw it.

The strangest character to write is the character for 'zero.' I had never considered it before, but the symbol for 'zero' in our Arabic numerals is a good one. An empty circle works well. It is simple, and effective. The Chinese symbol for zero, on the other hand, is written with sixteen separate strokes. And it looks like a strange and distorted picture of a man doing the splits.

The language also influences superstition. The Chinese think that it is very bad luck for two close friends or lovers to take a bite out of the same pear. The reason for this is rooted in the language: the word for “pear” is “li.” The word for “separate” is “fen li.” And so if you separate the pear between friends, then the friends will also part. It seems to be a slightly confused argument, and I don’t think that I fully understood it. But it seems to be an interesting concept nonetheless.

In Shanghai if you go to visit someone in hospital, you shouldn’t take them either pears (for the reason above) or apples. This is because the word for apple – “pingguo” – sounds (a little bit) like the Shanghainese word “bing gu,” which means death.

At weddings it is customary for the bride and groom to feed each other a bowl of food at their new home. This food is made up of dates, peanuts, dragon eye fruit and lotus seeds. This bizarre combination of foods owes nothing to flavour, or even, as might be expected, to Chinese medicinal beliefs over aphrodisiacs. It is because if you take a part of the name of each of the ingredients, then you get the sentence “zao sheng gui zi,” which means, roughly “have children soon.”

There are many other instances of words or numbers being lucky or unlucky due to the characters that represent them. Four is often considered an unlucky number because it sounds like the word for ‘death.’ The leader of the Taiping rebellion (the bloodiest civil war in history, in which over 20 million people died – the Taipings controlled much of central China for a period of eleven years around 1860), Hong Xiuquan, ‘realised’ that he was the son of God and the younger brother of Jesus Christ, partly because of a similarity in the characters of his name and those of Jesus’ name in the Chinese translation of the Bible, given to him by an American missionary. In fact, his utter conviction that he was the brother of Jesus contributed greatly to his eventual downfall: the Western powers would have been very happy to support a Christian Empire to replace the weakened Qing Dynasty, but Hong Xiuquan wouldn’t deal with the Western powers as equals: he was Jesus’ brother, therefore, he reasoned, the Western powers should bow down and recognise him as their God. Unsurprisingly, Queen Victoria was not prepared to bow down to a provincial Chinese warlord, and support for him evaporated. Without this support, his rebellion was ultimately quashed.

The written language holds immense power. I suppose that the amount of time that is spent learning these characters and how they relate to one another could be one rather unromantic reason for why their thoughts and beliefs are preoccupied by the relationships between the two. But I find it a very beautiful way for these beliefs to be formed. It is as though they believe that their language has arisen out of some great and mysterious force, and that they must look for patterns within it to try to fathom this force.

Chapter 12

By Thursday, I had barely left my desk for four days, and felt in dire need of a break. I donned my thermal vest, pulled a woollen hat down over my ears and prepared to shiver my way into town. But as I stepped out of the dormitory and into the sunshine, I was surprised by an almost warm breeze. It can't have been much more than 3 or 4 degrees above zero, but to me it was a heat wave, and I was determined to enjoy it. I tore off my hat, unbuttoned my shirt and strode off for Longsha Park.

Summer really did seem to have arrived in the park. They were burning piles of leaves by the waterside that produced that bonfire smell which seemed to promise an evening full of Pimm's and croquet and barbecued sausages. If I tried hard enough I could pretend that the distant hum of the traffic was just a few of the neighbours out mowing their lawns. Only the slowly dripping heaps of shattered ice-sculptures left over from the ice-festival remained as a reminder of the grim winter.

It may just have been the warmth of the day, or it may have been the contrast to the rest of the city, but the park seemed enchantingly beautiful. There is a vast man-made lake at one end called Labour Lake, and weaving back from this is a maze of tributaries that have been dug to feed the lake from the main river. In between these patches of water is a collection of lightly wooded strips of land connected to each other by arching bridges. There is a small hill topped by a five-story pagoda. All of this is fairly new – the pagoda is only a couple of years old. But it has been done tastefully. For once. Ambling through the park I saw the usual collection of elderly men and women practicing tai chi, and a bewildering number of people walking backwards. I later found out that they do this because of a belief that every step that they take backwards will allow them to take an extra one forwards, thereby prolonging their lives. It works on the same shaky principle as winding back the mileage on your car so that it will last longer.

And then I came to the zoo. Animals were packed in to such small cages that I found myself wondering if they had just been boxed up for transport. A couple of tigers chased their tales around a cage too small for them to take a full stride in any direction. In the wolf box, one of the wretched creatures simply turned around and around while the other did it's best to tolerate the woman who was poking it with a sharp stick through the bars. I felt an overpowering urge to tear down the flimsy wall of the cage and let the beast savage its tormentor. But I know how these things work, and it would doubtless be me who was torn limb from limb and left as a bloody mess on the concrete. And the sight of a foreigner being devoured would surely be more amusing to the locals than even jabbing a dog with a sharp stick. So I moved quickly on before the urge resurfaced. The next cage contained a simply enormous bird which I was unable to identify (although my being unable to identify it means, more or less, that is wasn't a pigeon, a pheasant or an ostrich) which was engaged in a fun little game with an old man. The old man had to jab the bird on the wing and try to grab a feather. The bird had to wait until he tried, then peck like mad and try to take his hand off. I must assume that the bird was a willing participant in this sport, because small though its cage was, it could easily have moved out of reach of the old man, had it so desired. I watched intently for about ten minutes, during which time the old man seemed to have the best of the play. He brandished four feathers, while the bird had yet to remove a single of his fingers. At last I despaired of the bird's chances, and skulked off. The only mercy was that the elephant that was brought here a couple of years ago had already died. It used to be chained up by all four legs so that it could barely move. With those enormous ears designed to keep it cool in the African savannah, it didn't survive its first Manchurian winter. Was anyone actually surprised?

I left the park, and wandered back past what used to be a line of four and five storey houses. These were almost all reduced to rubble at the time that I arrived. Just one little shop remained, the three stories above it having been haphazardly removed, and it squatted beneath a heap of concrete and bricks, only its merry little sign declaring that is was still in business. Inside it was a sad little place, the shelves almost empty except for a few packets of noodles, and a family of five sitting around on the floor looking glum. I tried to start a conversation with them, but though they were friendly, I was able to do little more than tell them that I was English, so I was unable to find out about their situation. I know that in Shanghai there are many similar situations where the people in question are refusing to move because the compensation that they have been given is so pitiful. Normally there the families are taken from an inner city location surrounded by all their friends, and resettled in apartment blocks in the suburbs where they know no one. Their society is torn apart and, especially for the old, this can essentially mean that their lives are torn apart. If I were to guess at this Qiqihaer family's predicament, it would be that they were being resettled in an apartment block, from where it would obviously be impossible to run their shop. So they would lose their livelihood as well as their home. In some ways it does need to be done though; there is no sanitation in these old buildings, and if it is to become the thriving "Western style" city that they want it to become, then that must change. And in Qiqihaer the apartments in which people are resettled are, I was always told, of a high standard, and people are generally happy to move. It is just those who have a business that relies on the location that are protesting. I don't know how true this is though; it was always impossible to tell. Either way, the semi-demolished shop made a mournful sight.

Chapter 13

That Saturday night, I went to a nightclub. The décor brought to mind a run-down fifties American diner and the music was just as rubbish as you would expect. But it was the clientele that made the place truly unbearable.

Theo had promised that he would join us at the club, but after twenty minutes it didn't seem likely that he would. I was feeling tired and awkward, and decided to make my excuses to the hoard of Russian girls, and head for the door. One of the Buriat girls, Maksara, was equally bored by the club, and came with me. We got ourselves a taxi, and were about to get in, when a man came tearing out of the club pursued by a silent crowd of thugs brandishing what looked to be truncheons. I wasn't sure for a moment whether they were playing some sort of game. But their silence was too threatening. Then they ripped the guy's shirt off, kicked him to the ground just in front of our taxi, and started beating him with the 'truncheons.'

He managed to scramble to his feet, duck between his attackers and slip between the taxi and me. A wave of his pursuers were bearing down on me, and I thought for a foolish, heroic moment about using my superior bulk to slow them down and aid him in his escape. But the headlights of a passing car flashed for a moment off the metal of their 'truncheons,' showing them to be knives, and I dived into the safety of the car. There were about twenty men with knives. I still couldn't see much blood on the victim's body, which was strange considering the number of times he had been slashed. I can only assume that the knives were blunt, or that most of the blows were to his head. They caught up with him again and beat him to the ground, where they continually stamped on his head. He broke free again, and was caught again. By now his hair was thick with blood and there was blood on the road. I assumed that if twenty people decide to go at somebody with knives, then they don't have any intention of leaving him alive, and thought again about what I could do. But at this point the aggressors stopped, and swept back towards our taxi, which we were now safely inside, but which was still frustratingly refusing to move. They surrounded us for a moment, laughing and waving their knives in a menacing way, but moved on. The man on the ground pulled himself up, and astonishingly seemed able to walk. He stood in the road trying to hail a taxi, and that was the last I saw of him. I tried to suggest helping him, but then Maksara said "don't trouble trouble 'til trouble troubles you." And with that we drove off. I felt pathetic and helpless for not doing anything, but I don't know what I could have done; I couldn't have spoken to him (at least if he wanted to talk about things other than what University he studied at, which I assume he would have done) and even if I could have done, I don't know what I could have offered. I had never witnessed such violence before, and never felt so useless. Joseph later told me that it was probably Mafia, and that either he would have been someone who owed them money, or he would have screwed some people over, who would then have paid the Mafia to teach him a lesson. Apparently this is often the way that people deal with situations in which they feel that have been wronged; the law courts are too corruptible. This is a more direct method.

Chapter 14

Towards the end of that fifth week, it struck me that I had totally adjusted to life in the foreign dormitory. I did not even notice the flickering lights in the passages anymore, and yet they were actually quite bizarre. They were dim at the best of times, and they went out completely every few minutes; you had to shout to make them go back on. No one seemed to know if this was a design feature, or merely a coincidence of a fault in their crap design that happened to be rectifiable by the making of a loud noise. Each passage had its own functional frequency: the fourth passage where the Austrians live required more of a shriek, whilst the lights on my own corridor required a more manly timbre to the voice. The building resounded every evening with shrieks and shouts every few minutes, and whilst as a fresh faced newcomer to the foreigners dormitory I had jumped with alarm and imagined with horror what evil tortures could be eliciting these noises, now I just thought wistfully to myself as I sat studying at my desk "ah, that sounds like the lights going out on the seventh floor again," and got back to work.

Only now did I start putting posters up in my room. I had been wrestling with yet another subconscious rule from my upbringing that didn't allow me to stick things to the wall with tape. At boarding school, this was utterly illegal: "it takes off layers of paint, and generally makes the place look messy," I remember being told. I had used up my meagre supply of blu-tack on sticking up the map, and so until now that had been the only decoration in my room.

Quite why that reluctance to stick things up remained when I was living in a room with walls that were coated in the graffiti of previous occupants I don't know. As for the idea that I may remove some of the paint, well that was just risible. There only was paint on about half of the wall, and even there it was mottled by chips in the concrete and holes drilled by some half hearted DIY enthusiast, through which ran bundles of apparently pointless wires. It had taken five weeks, but I had at last got over that mental block that ten years of school had drummed into me.

One thing that I was sad to be becoming accustomed to was the morning television. Not known anywhere in the world for being a highbrow cultural experience, the Chinese stuff really does stand-alone. But it holds a curious allure due to its total incomprehensibility. I had spent many amused hours watching traditionally costumed old men shouting amicably (not something that is possible to do in any language but Chinese) at each other over a cup of tea or some other such unfathomable nonsense. But one morning while watching a group of tartan clad Chinese girls demonstrating how to dance a foursome reel to the tune of 'Jingle Bells,' I was alarmed to notice myself not laughing. This could have been a result of the dull thudding in my head that always accompanies waking up after a night of baijiu, but I think that the main reason must have been that I just didn't notice those things as being peculiar any more. I was used to it. A light went out in my life with the passing of this innocent amusement, and I mourned it bitterly.

Chapter 15

Having experienced the unpleasantness of a weekend out on the town in Qiqihaer, I was keener than ever to get away at the end of my seventh week. I had planned to go alone, but when Jim and Heather heard that I was going to spend the weekend in a yurt in Inner Mongolia, they asked to join me.

So Friday evening saw the three of us strutting down the platform, bustling through the crowd and the smoke and the steam as uniformed guards checked underneath the trains with torches. It seemed a rather bizarre quirk of history that the Tsar's vision of a rail network spanning his great Siberian empire should have resulted, a hundred years later, in our being able to indulge in a long weekend break in Inner Mongolia. But it was the Chinese section of his great railway that would whisk us from Qiqihaer, to Manzhouli, on the border between Mongolia, Chinese Inner Mongolia, and Russia. The glamorous history combined with my mental image of Mongolia as a wild and untamed land to create a weekend of endless possibility and adventure. We found our cosy little cabin in the exclusive "soft seater" carriage, and settled down to an early night. Despite the comforting motion of the train, I was kept awake by my excitement as my imagination ran wild over the possibilities of the weekend.

At four o'clock I got up to have a look around. I left our cabin and shut the door quietly behind me, not wanting to wake Jim and Heather. I stumbled down the carriage to the large window at the end where, by the light of the full moon, I saw the menacing outline of a hill. It was not a big one, but it was the first rise of more than about twenty feet that I had seen for over a month. It held promise of great things to come. I tiptoed back to bed contented, and was finally able to sleep. I dreamed happily of days spent riding horses up mountains through the melting snow and down river valleys.

On arriving in Manzhouli, we found, after some difficulty, the person who had agreed by telephone the day before, to take us to a Mongolian yurt for a feast and to spend the night. She took us to a very expensive and very tacky hotel and checked us in. I couldn't understand a word of her English, but it seemed that we were not going to be actually able to stay in the yurt for the night, and could only go there for a meal. This was a crushing disappointment, but we took it in our stride, consoling ourselves with the thought that, after a day's horse riding, it might be nice to get back to a proper hotel and have a good bath.

Next, we were dragged to a 'French Bakery' for a soggy breakfast of pretend pizza and instant coffee, and were told that there were no horses either. And no camels. In an attempt to mollify us, she said that she would, for no increase in price, take us on a tour of the area herself. She had hired a taxi for the weekend, and would start by taking us to the famous lake, as soon as we had finished our breakfast.

"The lake will be frozen," observed Heather.

"Yes," nodded our guide excitedly.

"So there will be nothing to do," added Heather.

"No," agreed the guide, looking at her shoes, "there won't."

Only twenty-four hours earlier, when we had been back home in Qiqihaer, this same woman had assured us over the telephone that there would be no problem in riding horses and feasting and staying in yurts. Now a taxi ride to a frozen lake was the best that we were being offered.

We paid off the taxi that had been hired for us, and persuaded the guide to leave us alone. We were miserable, but determined that we would try to find some fun on our own.

After an hour or so of asking anyone that we could get to understand our stilted Chinese, we found a taxi driver who claimed to know a place where we could ride camels. He turned out to be as unreliable as our first guide. We paid copiously to be taken out to a summer camp of concrete yurts, bedecked with brightly coloured flags and peopled with 'real' Mongolians, who disappeared on our arrival to go and pull on some gaudy nylon versions of their national dress. We ate some dried and then overcooked meat with some salty sauces, and then went outside to be led in a small circle around the scrubby field on an unhappy camel by a man singing what, we were assured by a crew of nodding and beaming Chinese, was a genuine Mongolian folk song. I was lucky enough to be able to repeat the exercise on a barely living horse with a non-existent saddle.

Later that evening, we finally managed to achieve something like entertainment by rolling some cigars in our room using tobacco purchased in the otherwise utterly disappointing market. To round off a truly crap day, we went down to our sickeningly overpriced bar, brought some horrid whisky, and tried to smoke our disgusting creations.

The next morning I boarded the same train as Jim and Heather, but while they were going on a hard sleeper all the way back to Harbin, the ex-Russian concession on the Trans-Siberian Express, I was taking a hard seater only as far as Hailar – only five or so hours down the track. It was just getting dark as I left them and set out, alone once more, into the mystery of Hailar.

I had not enjoyed Manzhouli. I hated the oppression of the 'guide,' and I hated the disappointments of our little group. I always find that it is easier to suffer disappointments alone than in a group. If I had been on my own and my plans had been dashed, I would have shrugged and gone and found something else to do. It was the fact that Jim and Heather were so cut up about it that really got me down. I felt responsible for making them come all this way, and it made it hard just to change the plan.

Now that I was alone once more in Hailar, everything seemed rosier. I managed to buy myself the slowest possible ticket back to Qiqihaer; a hard-seater leaving the next day at 2.30pm and taking the best part of 20 hours, but until then I had nowhere to stay, nothing to do, and no one to do it with.

The next morning I woke early in the hotel that a kindly taxi driver had found me. In a series of compelling feats of linguistic ability and amazing luck, I managed to find a guide before 10 o'clock who seemed confident of finding me a yurt for lunch, and a horse on which to gallop through the meadows of the grasslands. With all this organised, I decided to miss my train, and to chase the yurt dream a little further. Although the guide knew almost no English, he did speak Japanese, so I had to pay the price of a 'translator' guide. Our communications were in a mixture of, on his part, Japanese, Chinese, Mongolian, appallingly pronounced English and a strange form of sign language involving a great deal of pointing at his nose with a curled index finger, and on my part, Chinese. I stubbornly refused to speak any English because this was the first occasion on which I could be fairly sure that my Chinese was better than his English, and I was damn well going to make use of the practice time.

"Macama!" he repeated, pointing at a wooden hut that we passed on our way out of the city and making explosion noises. I guessed that this was where the Japanese had made their tunnels when this was their Western frontier with Russia. I remembered reading about them in my guidebook (which I had cleverly left at home in Qiqihaer).

“Who…,” I asked, trying to feign an interest and so keep the conversation going, “were the Japanese fighting? The Chinese, or the Russians?”

“No! No! Macama!” he repeated. Pointing more urgently, and using his arm to represent someone being knocked over.

“Hmmm. We seem to have a bit of a misunderstanding here,” I thought to myself, “and there is that curious “macama” word again. It sounds a bit like “magma,” the way he is saying it.” I continued pointlessly rambling to myself as I became resigned to never understanding what he was on about, and started to drift off to my own little world.

“Fujisan!” broke through my peaceful dreaming. “Fujisan! Macama!” followed by more pointing at the wooden hut.

“So it *is* magma that we are talking about,” I thought. “There is some connection between a volcano in Japan and this small wooden hut in Inner Mongolia.”

“Boom,” I shouted, and motioned a volcano exploding. But it was more just for the limited fun of it than because I thought that I would learn anything more. He nodded happily, pleased that I now understood, and went back to chatting with the driver. I turned back to the hut and wondered absently what all this could be about. Like so much that I had seen and been told over the last month or so, I didn’t think I would ever really know.

It became clear after an hour or so that there really was nothing remotely organised about this tour, and I started to perk up. We poked around a big holiday camp set up, but found only a large gaggle of geese and a few turkeys squawking in a concrete mock-fort, which stood just set apart from the concrete mock-yurts. So we left this place behind, and set off once more into the wilderness. After another half-hour, my guide decided that he had spotted a yurt just over the hill. The problem was that on either side of the track there was a heavy build up of snow. This gave way to deep ruts of mud in places, and was clearly impassable, even to our plucky little Volkswagen Santana (which had already distinguished itself in terrain that would have made most Land Rovers uncomfortable). So the guide and I hopped out and set off on foot. It now occurred to me quite how little my guide had been expecting to spend his day thus engaged: he was neatly turned out in a suit, and his feet were protected from the mud by a natty pair of Chelsea boots. He picked his dainty little way from patch of ice to patch of ice, his toes pointed and his limp wrists flapping as he struggled to keep his balance, his whole manner entirely unbecoming of one who claimed to have been weaned on the life of a nomad. We passed a spot where the outlines of three yurts could clearly be seen on the grass; the yurts themselves had long since moved on. But at last, over the hill we found a motley collection of caravans, tents, and a tiny yurt. I had never actually seen a real yurt before; the closest I had come was one of the marquees at the New College ball in Oxford. But that one was far more realistic than this tosh that I saw before me now, on the plains on Inner Mongolia. It was tiny, for a start. It had a metal structure, instead of the wood that I knew to be traditional. And instead of traditional quaint Mongolian artefacts littering the inside, there were a couple of rubbish metal beds of the type popular in prisons, a wooden dresser, and a lamb, snooping about the place and bleating in a meaningless way. Of this, only the lamb was something that I had been remotely prepared for, and so was pleased to see. I was also gratified to learn that my host did not speak any Chinese, as this tallied with my “ethnic Mongolian” ideal, and so I put my disappointments to one side, and got on with the onerous work of gulping down airag (fermented mare’s milk) and trying to nod enthusiastically in the name of cross-cultural understanding. I did my best to look delighted by the Mongolian cheese; the worst cheese in the world, I would bet. I have eaten more tasty and toothsome lumps of rock. The lady of the ‘house’ arrived, and started dutifully to pull a gaudy nylon ethnic costume over her Adidas tracksuit, but I looked sufficiently uninterested, and thankfully she gave up.

It turned out that their horses were elsewhere at the moment, and the cheese was the only "food" (if I can dignify it with that description) that they had to offer, so we were compelled to move on. Guido (as he insisted on referring to himself) spoke of another camp at which he knew there to be horses, and where he suspected we would be able to eat lunch. At least I am pretty sure that that is what he said to me. It was, of course, not what happened. We spent the next hour driving still further along the increasingly poor track into the depths of the grasslands, occasionally we would spot some roving herders, and Guido would rush over to them shouting, "I've got a foreigner here! He wants to ride your horse!" Tempting though this may sound, none of them rose to the bait.

They made a wonderful sight though; the clothes worn by the herders I saw did more or less conform to the ideal of Mongol costume that my imagination held, and they drove herds of well over a hundred horses. Quite where they were going, or where they were coming from, I will never know

By this time I was starting to feel really ravenous, having missed my breakfast. And although having had a Mongolian banquet just the day before, I was under no romanticised misapprehensions about how satisfying lunch would be, I did really need something. I made my feelings known to Guido, who seemed to be of a similar opinion, and we turned the taxi around. Just as we reached the main road, we passed a farm with a lone horse tied up outside it. Guido wasn't going to miss this opportunity to fulfil the letter of his contract, and within a few minutes I had been led on my second circle-in-a-small-field experience in as many days (third, if you include the camel ride). I registered my disappointment in the only way that my language skills would allow: when he asked if it was my first time on a horse, I weakly lied that I had many horses at home, hoping that this would let him know that I had been dreaming rather more of the galloping-across-plains sort of riding, and less of the being-led-around-farmyards sort. I fear that any chance that this lie had of being believed was destroyed by my awkward "I have never ridden a horse in my life" posture and panicked clutching onto the mane for dear life. I made some weak efforts to excuse this incompetence through gesticulated protestations about the shape of the Mongolian saddle.

After the predictably disgusting lunch, at which I was once again forced to drink enormous quantities of baijiu, I was deposited at the market. By now quite tipsy, and having spent the whole day arranging things in Chinese, I was full of confidence in my abilities, and toured the stalls in a whirlwind of jocular exchanges. I promised to teach people's daughters English; I even promised to take one man to England with me. In a fishing shop I tried, with some limited success, to arrange a fishing trip in May. In other stalls, I used the "I'm not American" haggle, and sometimes it even worked. I bought a three-quarter litre hip flask just because it was amusingly big. Then I bought a faux leather pork-pie hat, I'm not quite sure why. But the whole thing was more about speaking in Chinese than buying anything actually useful. My aim was to go into the stall, ask about a few things, answer a few questions, and get out again before anyone noticed that I was really crap at Chinese. I played about twenty, won, I guess, about four, but only had two major thrashings. I felt pretty pleased about the whole thing, and made off for the station in a happy frame of mind.

I had missed my original train, and now upgraded to a hard sleeper that would get me in to Qiqihaer for an early breakfast. As I lay, slightly drunk, on my cramped top bunk, I reviewed the weekend and tried to write in my notebook.

"It has been a total failure in so many ways, and yet, what could I really have expected?" I scrawled. "I have the memories of the yurt. The memories of the Mongol herders driving horses across the plains. And no doubt in time my memories will take on some aspects of my unfulfilled dreams: the few painfully trotted steps across an icy farmyard will become 'galloping across the grasslands,' the yurt will start to resemble that at the New College ball, and I will have everything I wanted. What does it matter if it didn't actually happened like that? It was close enough in some ways. What *would* make it a 'genuine cultural experience?' If the woman in the yurt had put that ridiculous jacket on? Or if I had tried to gallop a bit? Or if I spoke Mongolian? I guess I got all that I could really ask for. And how many weekends do you come away from with a faux leather pork-pie hat and a three-quarter litre hip flask? Oh, and a bag full of Mongolian cheese – a gift from some nomads in a yurt, where I stopped for some airag whilst touring across the Hulunbuir grasslands in a Volkswagen Santana. Does it matter that it was disgusting?"

Chapter 16

Whatever I wrote at the time, the trip had been a disappointment. Back in my room, I drew a black line on my map, tracing the railway line from Qiqihaer south to the turn off, then north west through Hailar and on to Manzhouli. Even now it looked like a wonderful route, in spite of what I knew. I couldn't make the line on the map equate to the railway line I had travelled. After this slightly depressing realisation, I couldn't muster the enthusiasm to plan another trip for a while, and decided instead to spend the next three weeks in Qiqihaer, studying and trying to make friends with Chinese people.

My first effort at making a Chinese friend did not get off to a good start. George had asked me if I would mind helping a friend of one of his students to practice her English. She was planning to go to Nottingham University for a year, and needed to pass an English exam before she went. I would help her with her English for half of the time, and she would help me with my Chinese for the other half.

After finding out that her English name was 'Ardis,' that her parents lived in Qiqihaer, and that she was at University in Dalian, conversation ran a bit dry. I decided to find out what she knew about Nottingham, and why she had chosen to go there.

"Do you know anything about the history of Nottingham?" I asked.

"No." I tried some Robin Hood references, and got the excited reply "This jumper! He is from Robin Hood!" She searched for the label to show to me. I choked back my irritation that even this most popularised of "historical" figures should be known only as a make of clothing, and tried another tack.

“Are there any other places that you would like to go in England?”

“Yes.”

“Where?” The conversation was still not flowing.

“ Leeds.”

“For Christ’s sake,” I thought. “Why?” I said.

“They have a football team.”

“For Christ’s sake,” I thought. “Do you like football?” I said.

“No.”

“For Chris…” and so on. But this conversation was going, as you can see, nowhere, so I decided to move back to China. I had been fostering an interest in Chinese painting for a while, and asked her if she had ever done any painting. To my delight, she said that she had been a very keen painter when she was young, but that she had had to give up because she now had piano lessons instead.

“But do you still paint in your spare time?” I asked.

“No” she replied, looking confused, and then repeated, “now I have piano lessons instead.”

“But you could still paint without having lessons, couldn’t you?”

“No.” It was clear to me that we would never be great friends.

My next effort at making a Chinese friend came when, for some strange reason, I decided to give my real telephone number to one of the annoying students that hung around outside the foreigners’ dormitory asking for language partners. He seemed an irritating sort: very bouncy and slightly too pleased with himself. But I had promised myself that I would try to make some more Chinese friends, and after the failure of the lunch with Ardis, I would have tried almost anything.

The next day he called me, and we went for lunch together. Shaun had a 'bubbly' personality – and I mean that in the most disapproving way – but like all those who have taught themselves to speak English, I found myself oddly impressed by him.

His father left to go to Korea where he started a new family when Shaun was about fourteen. He offered to take Shaun with him and to give him a car and various other attractive offers, but Shaun didn't want to leave his mother on her own, so he stayed in Qiqihaer. He hasn't heard from his father since, and if you ask about him, Shaun will probably tell you that he is dead. To make some money, he left for the South when he was fifteen in order to (and I use his own words) "chase his dream" of becoming a professional pool player. He did this for a few years, more or less scraping by; he won a couple of competitions as a reward for which his patron bought him some really very well cut suits that he still wears every day. Eventually, since he wasn't really getting anywhere, he decided to teach himself English, and to see where it took him. He now works as a guide in Harbin in the winter and in Hangzhou in the summer. But his family is still in Qiqihaer, so he comes back here quite often. His English is better than any of the University students who are studying English; at least those that I have met. But since he never went to University, and has no English qualification, it is very difficult for him to get any job that involves using English. He needs the piece of paper in order to get the job. It must be frustrating for him, and yet he remains unnervingly jolly.

Shaun was keen to show me around Qiqihaer, but he didn't think that there was anything worth seeing. I tried to explain to him that it may all seem very normal to him, but to me Qiqihaer was an alien world, and the smallest market could fascinate me for hours.

“Do you like dwarves?” he asked. I stared back in dumb confusion. Just what was he asking me?

“I am not sure what you mean,” I tentatively replied.

“Dwarves. Small people,” he gestured with his hand, “Do you like?”

“I have no special feelings either for or against dwarves, Shaun,” I said diplomatically, and hoped that we could move on.

“But at the bathhouse they have dwarves that fight!” He nodded in excitement.

“Fight?”

“Yes! They have a stage and the dwarves box each other!”

“There is a stage in the middle of the bathhouse, and dwarves box each other on it?”

“Yes!”

“When can we go?” I had never heard of a more extraordinary scenario, and I felt that I must witness it.

So it was that I found myself having dinner with Shaun again just two days later, before heading on to catch the evening performance of boxing dwarves at the bathhouse.

We went to a traditional Korean restaurant where we took our shoes off and sat cross-legged on the floor of a mock kang: a raised room with coals underneath that heats the floor and causes the polythene table cloth to billow up in the warm draught. To my delight, the only meat on the menu was dog: I find there is something very rare and therefore rather wonderful about having my uninformed stereotypes confirmed. I'm not sure if I would have been happy to eat it though, and luckily I didn't have to decide: Shaun announced that he was not prepared to, so we went vegetarian for the evening.

Having used up all of my standard small talk on our first lunch, but having still not really discovered any common interests, I once again resorted to talking about all of my current hobbies, and seeing if any of them raised a flicker of interest from Shaun. I had found on some maps that there was a piece of wall near here that was marked with the same symbol as the Great Wall of China. I had become fascinated by this distant and unconnected fragment of wall, and asked if he knew anything about it. To my surprise, he had not heard anything about it. I decided that this was an invitation for me to explain, and, glad to have an audience for my research, I had just started to gabble happily about 'Liao dynasty defensive ditches,' when he cruelly crushed me with a drab "I am not interested in History. It is Boring." I stopped, my face reddening, and wondered again how the Chinese can be so totally disinterested in their awesome history. I decided to argue the point.

"Why do you think history is boring?"

"For China now, the future is exciting. The past is bad, and is of no use. In the future, China will be great. In the past, things were difficult. So we like to talk about the future and not about the past. Maybe for you English, the past is better than the future, so you like to talk about the past." I don't know if he meant it as a put down, but it stopped me in my tracks quite effectively. I don't actually agree with it as an explanation either; I think that the British were always interested in history, even when we were at the start of our empire. But it certainly stopped me thinking of him as a friendly but uneducated failed pool player.

He wasn't as belligerently pro-China as most of the University students that I have met; he spoke of bad things as well as the good things about the country. He told me that a few years ago in Qiqihaer, a group of local youths had got hold of SCUBA diving equipment, and gone diving in the river. When other people came out swimming past them, these youths would grab them and pull them under water, holding them there until they drowned. They would then hide the body at the bottom of the river, and wait until the family of the deceased started trying to find it so that their beloved could be given a proper burial. Then they would advertise their services and, for a reasonable fee, recover the body.

"This sort of thing, it happens in China. I don't think it happens in your country." I hoped not.

Over dinner Shaun broke the terrible news that the boxing dwarves had left town to continue their tour of the country, and the entertainment at the bathhouse would therefore be something much less extraordinary. I was sorely disappointed, but having nothing else to do, I thought that I might as well go along.

For some reason I still had in my mind a sepia-tinted image of the baths in which hundreds of people stood draped in towels in a steam-filled stone hall gazing up at a rickety wooden stage on which two pint sized pugilists fought tooth and nail. Immediately on arriving at the bathhouse, however, it was clear that I had once again dreamed wide of the mark; the foyer was bedecked in marble and gold that seemed altogether too gaudy to fit with my old fashioned dream. But I had suffered larger upsets before, and I resolved to sit back and see what happened.

I will admit to being somewhat reserved when it comes to matters of nudity. My heart sank as I was led down a mirrored corridor that was serving as a barber's studio, and into a nest of fat naked Chinese men that served as the changing room. I devoted an elaborately large amount of time to undoing my slip-on shoes, and spent another panicked few moments pretending to be interested in the padlock that secured my locker. Painfully slowly I started to unbutton my shirt, I removed one arm and then the other, and when it was finally off, I folded it neatly before carefully tucking it into the locker. All the while I wondered whether it would be more embarrassing to be wearing nothing, or to be the only one wearing swimming trunks. And I prayed for some sort of reprieve. Of course, none came. At last, and to a gathering crowd, I removed my shorts and stood stark naked, except for a clean white flannel that had been issued to me at the front desk, and which I now held clumsily in one hand, wondering how effectively I could use it to hide my genitals, without letting on that I was feeling in the slightest bit awkward about the whole nudity thing.

The answer of course was not effectively at all. But years of private showering got the better of me, and I was unable to stop my arm from drifting across at an awkward angle, letting the flannel drape daintily over the area in question. I tried a few bold "ah, I'm really very comfortable with this situation" steps, but I doubt I fooled anyone. In fact in hindsight, I doubt anyone cared. But I cared; I was watching my actions with critical scrutiny, and everything I saw made me worry still more.

"Damn it," I thought, "look at the way your limp little wrist is draping that stupid flannel! You look like a mincer! Now *they* are all feeling awkward, they think you are eyeing them up! Keep looking at eye level, don't stray downwards; don't look down. Damn..." Now that I consciously looked at their eyes, I saw that they were indeed staring at me. "Maybe they're staring at your hair… they've never seen a hairy chest before, pretend you don't notice, pretend you don't care." But I knew that they were not looking at my chest, and I only felt more awkward. "Stop that tottering waddle, it reeks of awkwardness! Take nice, casual swinging strides… Ow!" My casual stride took me into a sharp bench at knee height. I was now surrounded by ten or so of the fat naked audience, who put their big sweaty arms around me and gabbled in Chinese, whilst I hopped around clutching my knee, swearing wildly, but still wafting the pathetic little towel between my legs, ludicrously hoping that this in some way could save my 'dignity.'

Eventually I overcame these teething difficulties, and after a quick and unpleasant visit to the sauna, I actually managed to gain some fleeting pleasure from hopping into the cold bath. Flushed with this success, and thrilled by the idea that I might in fact be able to enjoy this nightmare, I decided to give the hot bath a try. This seemed to be rather more popular with the locals, who had all looked rather shocked when I had gone for the cold water. I clambered over the limestone wall, and plonked myself down in a quiet corner of the green marble tub, just next to a green dragon sculpture that spewed out steaming water. Although by no means sepia-tinted, there was a gaudy luxury to the place that I was rather taken by.

These moments of tranquillity never last for long in China, and in a few moments I was surrounded by another herd of portly naked men, keen to chat. I tried my best to communicate, and managed to discover that one of them was an engineer at the train station. The plumpest of all of them started to talk to me about his hometown. I lost the gist of the conversation for a moment, and before I had a chance to catch up, he had leapt to his feet and begun a karate display of a kind that I sincerely hope I will never have to see again. His naked groin bounced just inches from my nose, and I was hemmed in on both sides so there was no escape. It turned out that he was from Shaolin: famous for the Shaolin monks who are the greatest exponents of martial arts.

At this point Shaun reappeared, announced that the show was about to begin, and that we should head upstairs. I leapt out of the tub and bolted for the changing room without so much as a backward glance.

Back in the locker room, I was issued with a disposable pair of briefs that seemed to have been fashioned from the material used to sit hunks of meat on in supermarket packages. An hour before I would have laughed at the idea that I would ever put such a thing on, but now I was far enough gone to think "sod it" with a resigned shake of the head, and squeeze into them. It wouldn't have surprised me if we were expected to attend the performance wearing only these semi-transparent pouches. But it was not to be. We were all also issued with identical sets of blue and gold cotton pyjamas. As I later discovered when we went upstairs, the girls were all issued with identical sets of pink frilly meringues, which I think were possibly even more offensive.

The entertainment hall itself had none of the Old World charm of the rickety stage that my imagination had created. Instead it was the very model of what the club class lounge on a cross channel ferry should be. There was a thick blue carpet with heavy floral patterns. Enormous padded chaise-longue stood in rows three deep around the edges of the room. After the show had finished, when we were making to leave, I noticed that many people remained, apparently asleep, curled up underneath their duvets.

"They sleep the night here," Shaun told me "It is for free."

In the centre of one side of the room, there was the stage; a glitzy raised platform on which Bruce Forsythe would have felt quite at home. Directly in front of this, there was the table-seating area where drinks were served. This is where Shaun and I headed. The floor was glass, and beneath my feet I watched a skinny woman fighting a rubber ring in the swimming pool.

Two long-haired gothic-looking youths sporting 'megerdearth' (sic) t-shirts were sat on high stools brandishing guitars on either side of the stage. The house lights went down, the spotlights came on, and a drum solo erupted. The 'megerdearth' lads then joined in, thrashing their strings and producing a noise that, even through the heavy distortion that they were using, was instantly and bizarrely recognisable as that annoying tune that some clocks play when striking the hour and that has been hijacked by tasteless doorbells all over suburbia.

Over the next three hours I was subjected to some of the most miserable entertainment the world has to offer: seven stout girls dressed in puce green Victorian style dresses – but with the fronts cut away to reveal PVC miniskirts, lethargically ‘danced’ to tinny Chinese pop. Next came a boy band of failed gymnasts who sang poorly and occasionally performed a somersault. Their painfully over-rehearsed gig came across as lifeless even through the language barrier. These were replaced by a ‘magician’ who kept dropping her tricks, and smashing glasses before she ever managed to achieve anything remotely impressive. At this stage I lost interest and my eyes strayed over to the bar, where an affluent gent was being given a ‘fire massage’: what looked like hundreds of little octopus suckers were being set fire to and then fixed to his back. I watched transfixed for a few moments, and by the time I looked back, the dancing girls were back once more, this time dressed as nuns. They began with an austere candle lit ceremony before a change in the tempo of the music jerked them into an enthusiastic fit of leaping and bottom waggling. As they gradually became more synchronised, the stage started to bounce to their rhythm. Soon the glass floor on which I was sat was bucking like a bouncy castle. I shot a nervous glance towards the engineer that I had met earlier, but seeing that he was unconcerned, I blithely decided that I too would put my trust in it. I ‘enjoyed’ another moment of being the centre of attention, when a long haired head-banging singer with a pot belly and improbably spindly legs noticed me in the audience and instructed the spot to be turned in my direction so that the crowd could get a better look. I looked coyly down at my feet, beyond which I could see the skinny woman still fighting the rubber ring, blissfully unaware of the concert raging above her. But woven in with all this rubbish were the occasional touching and occasional truly depressing moments. One of the otherwise mediocre singers pulled out a recorder-like musical instrument used by her ethnic minority, and played some traditional songs of echoing beauty. A less pleasant sight was that of an upsettingly fragile contortionist tying herself in unimaginable knots and trying stoically to force her face into a smile. "Trained by tears," said Shaun.

When I dropped Shaun back at his house, he made me walk with him right to his door, because he is worried about the safety of the area (he had mentioned earlier that his local restaurant owner was stabbed to death last week). "I *am* a real man" he kept repeating earnestly, "it's just that one must be *safe.*" He either didn't seem to notice, or didn't seem to care, that I would be having to walk back on my own, in the dark, and that I was about (very roughly) a million times more conspicuous than him. But by that stage of the evening I had faced enough of my fears that a few knife wielding maniacs leaping from the shadows really seemed quite tame.

Chapter 17

My interest in painting was given a boost when Joseph found an art teacher called Barbarian who said that he was prepared to give me some lessons in return – as always – for me helping him with his English. He needed to pass an English exam before he was allowed to continue studying for his Masters.

The class was held in Barbarian's study: a cramped, high-ceilinged room with damp creeping across the walls. Four sturdy desks had been clumped together in the centre of the room to form the work surface and a collection of rickety chairs were wedged in between this and the walls. On one side of the room, behind the chairs, a shelf had been converted into a bed. As I entered, the previously quiet room erupted in a gaggle of "harrow!"s and "I pleased to meet foreign gentleman"s, which caught me slightly by surprise; I had been naïve enough to expect a one-on-one lesson. But it was not to be. Within moments a photographer had arrived, and snapped away keenly while I did my best to stop my face from drifting into the moronic discombobulated look that had become its repose.

Barbarian took charge, although it turned out that his level of English was really very low. He introduced all of the others using their English names.

"I Barbarian!" he said with the obvious glee of someone who knows that his audience will laugh. He flexed his arm muscles and did what I imagine was a well-rehearsed mime. "This," he went on, pointing to the man on his left "is *Professor* Martin Luther King, this is *Professor* William Wallace, this," pointing to the young girl next to me, "is *student* Man Friday, and this," his glee was even more pronounced than before, "is *Professor* James Bond!" We all howled with laughter while Professor Bond nodded happily. He was about sixty years old and rather serious looking. I am not sure whether he had chosen the name as a joke, or as a serious tribute to a great man. But he didn't seem offended by the laughter.

Traditional Chinese painting is very similar to traditional Chinese calligraphy. There are set ways of drawing everything and you must study these methods, learn them perfectly, and then put your own interpretations into them. The first bird that I learnt to draw, for example, was started with three short splodgy strokes that form the back of the bird. In total it takes about twenty or so strokes to do the whole bird.

"When you happy, the bird you paint is happy," James Bond kept repeating to me. I can sort of understand in principle what he means, but the reality of it is that these Chinese birds all have a pretty sinister crow-like appearance that reminds you of an Alfred Hitchcock creation and could not possibly, in my opinion, look anything other than rather scheming and bitter. Still, I dutifully copied his strokes, and presently had produced a rather squat and hunchbacked version of Bond's graceful beast. We continued the picture, adding lotus flowers and a mossy rock for the bird to perch on, until Bond judged it to be finished. His looked like quite a simple, but rather charming and well-balanced piece of art. Mine looked like a disjointed and talentless copy; which is, I suppose, exactly what it was. I tried to explain to them that mine just looked like a load of messy marks, and not like a picture at all, and much to my gratification, they nodded with excitement and informed me that this is one of the key points in Chinese art. They then started to explain a totally different point about realistic against abstract art, but I decided not to correct them; I was happy with the kudos I seemed to have gained through my supposedly incisive remarks.

I had another go at this drawing 'on my own;' although this in actual fact meant that whilst I did not have Mr Bond to copy each stroke from, I did have five vocal Chinese barking advice and instructions at me about everything from the length of stroke that I should make, to the amount of water on my brush in a bewildering combination of Chinese and English.

I liked the fact that there are still people prepared to spend the enormous amount of time and effort that it takes to learn all of the rules for this traditional art form. I had pessimistically supposed that all students now would be keener on pursuing the more easily accessible and more 'modern' western style of painting. But this group was a total mixture of ages, from Professor Bond at the top, down to William Wallace and Man Friday, who were both in their early twenties.

They also seemed to be a reassuringly rebellious group; what you would hope from a group of artists. Barbarian sported a daring ponytail (technically illegal in the University) and the others all dressed in a manner that could be considered to be making a statement. I like the fact that these sorts of people are learning the old skills. Although in all honesty, it is most likely determined by the University telling them what they can study. Very few of the students have any choice over their studies; they take an entrance exam and are told "right, you are good at Maths, so get on with it," regardless of whether they have any interest in it. So they were probably just told that traditional Chinese painting was all that was on offer, and so that is what they are stuck with. But if that is the case, then I, probably hypocritically, support the university in its authoritarian maintenance of tradition.

Over the next couple of weeks I had several more lessons, and started to be able to wield my brush in an almost tolerable way. Communication was sometimes strained, but I enjoyed the fumbling with electronic dictionaries and enthusiastic guessing that went into every conversation. I also looked through hundreds of books of paintings, and decided that the charmingly named 'White Snow Storm' (bai xue shi) was my favourite living traditional Chinese artist. He painted mountains of the jagged sort that typify Chinese painting for me. I don't know how exactly they do it, but these paintings have a sense of scale and grandeur that is always lacking in Western depictions of mountains.

When conversation was running a bit slowly one day, I decided to ask them about the mountains around Qiqihaer, hoping that they would tell me of some that I could visit. They said that there were no mountains anywhere near here that could be painted.

"What about in Inner Mongolia?" I suggested.

"No."

"But there are mountains there, aren't there?"

"Yes, but they are covered in trees, and so it is not possible to paint them." This was not an 'impossible' that meant 'very difficult,' it was an 'impossible' that meant 'the techniques we have do not extend to such things.' It seemed to me to be extraordinarily defeatist to not paint something just because you have not been taught exactly how to do it, but that is the way that Chinese painting works. There are techniques that are learned, and if those techniques do not tell you exactly how to paint something, then you just don't paint it.

On another day they spoke to me of how the Chinese had been painting abstract pictures for hundreds of years before the idea occurred to people in the West. Picasso had studied traditional Chinese painting and had taken many of his ideas from it, they claimed. I don't know if there is any truth in this, but I liked the idea. I liked chatting away to this bizarre collection of people, and I liked hearing their ideas about the world. I had great respect for all of them.

But in the third week of my lessons I arrived one morning to find only Man Friday and Martin Luther King were present. Martin looked awful, and Man Friday was clearly embarrassed.

“I am so sorry,” she began. “Barbarian, James Bond, William Wallace and Martin Luther King have been up all night playing ‘Counter Strike’ on the internet. They have all just gone to bed except Martin.”

“I am tired,” said Martin Luther King, and climbed up onto a shelf behind me where he was soon snoring loudly. I stayed and chatted with Man Friday for a few minutes, but she was only a student and therefore was not allowed to oversee my wielding of a brush. So I left, slightly riled by this group of University professors who had failed to turn up to a lesson because they had spent too long playing computer games. The respect that I had had for them had evaporated, and I never made it to another class.

Chapter 18

After about two months in Qiqihaer, my shoes started to disintegrate. This was a cause for some concern; Chinese shoes are rarely made in size eleven, and I was going to have a difficult time finding replacements. With the changing of the seasons, Stephen and Joseph wanted to buy some new clothes, so we set off together in search of the shops. We visited market after market, all crammed with disgusting articles of clothing and thousands of tiny shoes. There was nothing that could conceivably have been bought. Stefan seemed surprised by this. I, I must admit, wasn't; if there were nice clothes on sale in Qiqihaer, then you would expect to see at least some people wearing them, but you never did.

So that was a failure, and I resigned myself to wearing my walking boots for my remaining time there. But Joseph had been languishing with a broken leg for the previous four months, and so had not left the University for a very long time, so we were keen that our expedition into town would not be a complete failure. The only thing that there actually is to buy in Qiqihaer is DVDs. They are of variable quality, and all are technically illegal, but they are so cheap that you tend to overlook those points as details. We went to a little clutch of shops in a courtyard just off the main square.

In the first shop I found a copy of "Gladiator" that had the normal picture of Russell Crowe on the front, brandishing a sword. But next to him, instead of a picture of Oliver Reid, or one of the other characters, was a scantily clad young lady stroking her bosom in a seductive manner. I assumed that this was an amusing way of trying to sell a film that they felt to be slightly lacking in the romance department. Imagine my surprise, when I arrived at the counter to be told by a blushing spinster that this was an altogether more risqué version, in which Russell Crowe did not feature, and in which the young lady was swiftly to become entirely unclad (I, of course, didn't actually understand what she was saying, but could guess quite easily from her super-coyness, and by the time Joseph had translated for me, I was able to put on a suitably shocked display to convince them that this *really* was not my kind of film). Thus I was introduced to yet another seedy underbelly of Qiqihaer society; dealing in illegal porn films. There are only a few stores that sell them, and they are always 'disguised' in the clever way that had so confused me.

In the next shop, which was also one of the seedy porn dealers, we noticed a young Chinese couple skulking nervously next to the counter, and waiting for the other customers to leave. Everyone was at the other end of the shop except for Joseph, and assuming that he didn't understand Chinese, they finally plucked up courage to speak.

"Do you have any, err, *other* films" asked the young man.

"Eh?"

"*Other* films?"

"Ahh! Yes yes," The shopkeeper replied, reaching for a stack behind the till. "Here you are," and she began to read through the titles slightly more loudly than the nervous young man would have liked. The girlfriend turned a deep shade of red, and disappeared off to the other end of the shop.

"Also, we have a new exciting type" the lady advised him "this" she says, holding up a filthy-looking offering "is Karaoke porn!" Joseph spluttered, trying to restrain a laugh, and hobbled from the shop. Stephen and I rushed out after Joseph to check that he wasn't going to die, and when we all returned, we were laughing heartily and pretending not to stare at the unfortunate young man. By now, he was looking both embarrassed and confused. He was clearly as bemused by the concept of karaoke porn as we were, but was still to shy to ask.

Is it supposed to be a visual instruction guide? Or just a more traditional karaoke style; a porn video without the sound, but with lyrics at the bottom of the screen giving the male and female parts making suitable copulation sounds? Whatever it entails, the image of this blushing couple sitting rigidly on their sofa, watching this filth in, presumably, some sort of shocked silence, only broken by their alternate staccato muttering of the 'lines' being marked out in blue at the bottom of the screen was too much for us, and we had to leave the shop once again to cry with laughter out of sight of the unfortunate couple.

Outside we were approached by an old man. He was brandishing a piece of paper, and asking us our names. Joseph went first, and said his name a few times, before writing it down in order to show him the characters. Then Stephen wrote his name down. I then embarrassed myself by saying my Chinese name a few times, but being unable to tell him the characters.

"You write it down, Joseph." I told him, sure that he would know how do it.

"I *could,*" he replied, slightly sceptically, "but he wants you to write it; that is really the point of getting autographs." I stood in shocked silence. I have had my photo taken many times, but that is just a general factor of being a big-nose. Here this man was actually interested in *me* in particular, and wanted my *autograph.* I was honoured, and scrawled a flourishing signature across his scrap of paper.

"When you are all Presidents," he said, "this will be very valuable."

Chapter 19

As I walked over to my lunchtime restaurant one day in my eighth week in Qiqihaer, the morning's snow had turned to a persistent drizzle. I picked my way along the spurs of mud between the puddles, and felt curiously at home. It was good British weather, and I liked it. At the restaurant I then had to pick my way between the myriad of buckets and bowls that had been arranged in the entrance of the building to catch drips from the leaking ceiling. In one of these bowls a couple of bass thrashed hopelessly around, biding their time until they were eaten. Finally I arrived in the restaurant proper, and found George and his girlfriend Diana already eating. Diana's face was scrunched up in disgust as she protested that she had found something alive in her soup. The waitress was peering into her bowl while George implored her to wait a moment before removing it, while he found his glasses.

"I can't see anything in there. Are you sure? Hold on a minute. Anyway, it can't be alive; it's too damn hot in there!" he protested. Just as his spectacles reached his nose, the waitress's hand darted into the soup and emerged triumphantly brandishing a small white shrimp-like insect, it's legs still twitching. George's doubts over the alien's existence thus quashed, he turned to hearty cries of "it's extra protein!" that one will always hear when such unexpected creatures are found in one's food. Diana was still understandably reluctant to eat more of the soup, and ordered herself some rice. The waitress disappeared with the "shrimp," only to return from the kitchen a few moments later with a much larger example.

"Now this," she seemed to say "is a proper sized one. Not like that weedy little number you were complaining about." For a moment I looked suspiciously down at my plate of fish flavoured meat strips, and reconsidered my affection for my favourite eatery. But it was just a momentary lapse, and soon, with a cry of "it's all good nutrition," I tucked hungrily back in.

While Diana was still reeling from the experience, George's appetite for insect stories had been only been whet by the episode, and he eagerly started on another tale. He had been to the computer store the week before with some of Diana's friends who had a broken games console. They took it up to the counter, told the woman what was wrong, and asked her to mend it. She looked very wary; she clearly had a strong suspicion of what was to come. She walked out of her shop, and started to work away on the console in the hallway outside, tentatively jabbing with a screwdriver. After a few minutes jabbing, a couple of cockroaches shot out, and were stamped to dust by five enthusiastic students. "Ah," thought George, those cockroaches were screwing it up somehow," and he was right, in a way. The cockroaches were the problem, or at least part of it; they can eat up some of the wires, and generally make mischief. Where George was mistaken was in thinking that the two roaches that had emerged so far were anywhere near the whole problem. The brave technician continued her dissection of the console, and more and more roaches gave themselves up. The whole console was about the size of a cigar box. Eventually, when it was reduced to all of its tiniest constituent parts, the floor was covered in the squashed remains of over two hundred of the scuttling beasts. I never saw many cockroaches in my room, and I had always assumed that the cold winters must kill them off. But maybe I just never looked hard enough.

Chapter 20

Stephen had been having lunch with some Chinese, but he came over just as he was leaving, and gave me two tickets to a 'show' that was currently on at the stadium. I had noticed a large crowd there, bustling around yet another red-carpeted wooden stage filled with brightly dressed men and women, as I had passed by this morning on the bus. I had been too slow to be able to get off at that stop and investigate, and at the next stop I couldn't quite muster the interest to take the bus back. But with these tickets and Stephen's recommendation ("it is really crap, but you like that sort of thing, don't you?") I decided to make the trip.

The commotion that I had seen earlier outside the stadium turned out to be a raffle. I bustled about for a few minutes and tried to buy myself a ticket, but I couldn't work out who was selling, and who was just brandishing useless bunches of tickets. Then I saw a poor student being dragged up onto the stage and forced to answer a series of, clearly highly embarrassing, questions before he was allowed to take his prize, and I ditched my efforts; the tiny risk that I might win was still too great for me to play. It would be too awful. So I bypassed the raffle and went straight in to the main show.

The stadium was one of those big concrete blocks that some desolate town in Northern England might have put up in the 1960s. But you know that it has been used for hundreds of public executions, so it has an even more horrible atmosphere. There were no seats, so I cleared a space for myself amidst the sea of sunflower-seed shells on the hard steps and settled down to enjoy the show.

The single performer was dressed in bright nylon versions of some ethnic minority dress. His stage was a red carpet. In fact it was more of a small red rug, laid out on the edge of the football pitch. About twenty metres behind him there was a larger raised stage that inspired some hope of grander performances to come. Many times in the next hour this forlorn hope was the only thing that kept me there.

The first performance was this bright yellow man whimpering away in the local style of ‘rap.’ It is a strange singing style, in some ways reminiscent of Peking Opera, but sung on only one note, and with a very aggressive rhythm. I couldn’t understand a word of it, and it hurt my ears to listen. A big-haired woman joined him after a while, and together they sang an apparently amusing duet. It was an even more awful display than the bathhouse cabaret. But by now my mind was on other things. The performance was being aimed at one side of the stadium only, but with some swift arithmetic and a few guesses, I worked out that there must be over 3000 people here. Not that many, I suppose, but they were of all ages, and it was 2.30pm on a Monday afternoon.

“Don’t these people have jobs to be going to?” I thought. I suppose they didn’t. There are not very many ways that you are really made aware of a high unemployment rate; a rise in violent crime is one possible one, and people being free to go and watch crappy local rap acts on a Monday afternoon is another. But although I also didn’t have a job, I was not yet bored enough to waste entire afternoons watching that sort of drivel. So I fought my way through the unemployed crowd, and made for the park.

I hadn’t been to the park since that day when I had pre-emptively seen the arrival of summer heralded by the melting ice-sculptures. And I still hadn’t actually been inside the pagoda on top of the hill. So I clambered my way up there, passing on my way the only litter-picker-upper I have ever seen in China (“Poor woman,” I thought; a thankless and impossible task if ever there was one.) But I am glad that at least someone is trying. As I climbed, I was really quite amazed by what I saw: the pagoda itself became less impressive and more mundanely concrete with every step I took up the hill, but the view itself was striking. From here I could see all of the little waterways with their high-arched interlocking bridges laid out below me like a full sized version of those tiny Japanese gardens made with bonsai trees of which my grandmother is so fond. More pagodas seemed to float serenely on the lake, tethered by their pontoons. And then directly below the mound on which I stood, on the other side from the road, was the biggest surprise of all: a large Qing dynasty temple. It caught me completely unawares; I don't think that I had heard anyone mention it before. I decided to go and visit as soon as I had finished with the pagoda. But first, having come this far, I felt obliged to climb up as high as I could, so I crept up the spiral staircase, ducking to try to avoid banging my head. After the first twenty steps, I lost concentration, and a lower bit of ceiling caught me by surprise, thudding down my scull in that incomparable and sick-making way that bits of ceiling sometimes do. Just at this moment a jolly lad in cheesecake trousers shouted "harrow!" at me. It was all I could do to restrain myself from throwing him over the edge. But with a superhuman effort I blinked back the tears and climbed up another level. I took a couple of quick photos, and headed back down again. The "harrow"-er was on the second level to meet me, grabbing me with excitement and jabbering away. I already hated the poor guy, associating him, as I did, with the head-banging incident. But I did my best to be friendly.

I was perhaps too friendly in my efforts to disguise my true feelings, and what I had intended to be a quiet and solitary stroll around the park now turned into a whistle-stop tour of everything that Wang (as he turned out to be called) felt was of interest. The temple was beautiful, but I barely had time to appreciate it, so speedily was I dragged around. I was hauled into a quiet room containing large statues and cushions to kneel on as you prayed. Incense was burning, and I felt very awkward. I felt sure that I must have been imposing myself where I was not wanted. Everywhere I went, I heard mutters of 'da beizi' (meaning 'big nose;' it is the standard derogatory word for foreigner). So I made only a token effort to slow Wang down.

Another site that Wang showed me, though only by chance as it happened to be on the way to a part of the lake that he wanted me to see, was a large aeroplane being taken to pieces. "It's being changed," Wang said; though I suppose I misunderstood him. The fuselage stood pathetically alone, it had rolled slightly to one side and reminded me of one of those stubborn sausages on a barbecue that just won't sit straight. Surrounding it were its scattered wings and engines, all being teased apart with screwdrivers by swarms of old men in leather hats. Had I been on my own, I would have tried to engage some of these in conversation. But Wang had no interest in the plane; it was old. And so we rushed on to look at the peddle-boats. Wang was keen to take me to eat, although it was just past three o'clock, and so not a mealtime. The Chinese will always invite you to go for a meal rather than for a drink. If you are drinking, you are also eating. I had warmed to Wang a little after our bad start, but I still didn't feel like getting dragged into a full afternoon with him, so I claimed that I had a class to go to. I gave him my phone number and legged it for the bus.

Chapter 21

Jim managed to find a Qiqihaer tourist guide that had been printed in English in 1989 when someone seemed to hold genuine illusions that Qiqihaer would one day become a major tourist destination. It is a hilarious little book.

The front-page photograph shows a dreamy summer's day on a lake: leafy willow trees, ornate pagodas and romantic couples (presumably) reading poetry to each other in elegant boats. Longsha Park was the only place in Qiqihaer that was remotely similar to that photograph, and although the park is, as I had by then discovered, quite beautiful, it simply doesn't contain the same pagodas. It is a fantasy. But the lies don't stop there: once you get inside the book, you are repeatedly seduced with pictures of non-existent temples in imaginary gardens. I don't know if all of this *was* really here in 1989, and has since been hastily removed, or if this was published as a work of fiction. Some of the historical and cultural 'facts' were equally suspect. For example it claimed that the historic town of Tazi contained ruins built in the Zhou dynasty in the 11th century BC. If this was indeed the case, then it would dramatically change the traditional historical view backed up by every other piece of evidence in existence that the land governed by the Zhou dynasty stopped several hundred miles from here. When describing the Catholic Church in the city, they assure us that "Arabic is still used for conducting Mass." I'm no Catholic, but there seems to be something a trifle fishy about that sentence. But whatever it's faults, it *was* a Qiqihaer tourist guide, and I made it my mission to visit all of the sights that it suggested.

Zhalong Nature reserve is the most famous tourist attraction in Qiqihaer. In ornithological circles, it could almost claim to be world famous. I had previously read that it is home to nine of the world's fifteen species of cranes. This is the largest number that can be found in any one place in the wild. This tourist guide however described the Zhalong as having 14 of the world's 15 species of crane. I first assumed that this was just a lie, but on reading further I discovered, to my surprise, that it was in fact true; they had bought up all the other varieties of crane from all over the world (except one), and now kept them in cages at Zhalong. This seemed to me to be a strange way to run a Nature reserve.

These cages seemed, from the book, to be all that visitors were able to see: "Wild red-crowned cranes….are usually moving about in reed marshes some 25 kilometres away from visitors. Viewers can only see their beautiful images through telescopes." The red-crowned cranes are the ones that people most want to see, so they have kept them in cages to make it easier to get a look. I can follow the logic, but that doesn't mean that I agree with it.

Still more ridiculous is the description of the sport of "Crane Racing," accompanied by an absurd photograph: an assorted bunch of cranes of all different sizes being herded along a 'race track' by a group of uniformed officials, while about 20 bewildered locals look on in obvious boredom.

"Hence," the book concludes after a ten page torrent of crane-related information, "another name for Qiqihaer is 'City of Cranes.'" They don't seem to have been told by anyone that 'City of Cranes' brings to mind an image of a building site that, while accurate, is probably not what they intended.

Having read all about this bizarre nature reserve, I was convinced that it would be a very boring place to go. But I couldn't spend four months in the City of Cranes and never visit it once, so I intrepidly set off to see what I could find.

I was feeling thrifty, and was piously reluctant to fork out the 120 kuai that the taxi driver had told me it would cost to get to the reserve. I took a bus to the station, where after much asking around I managed to get a friendly old man in a leather cap to negotiate for a motor cyclist to give me a lift me to a local bus station just out of town. Once at the local bus station, I got to fold myself up like a deck chair and squash into the back seat of a diminutive little van; a seat that I happily shared with a smelly Chinese youth and what I hope, for the sake of morality, was his wife. They petted and groped away at each other, more or less in my lap, while I tried to suspend my mind and look distantly out of the window. Beyond the lines of silver birches that traced the road on either side, horses ploughed fields littered, as ever, with brightly coloured plastic bags. Old men smoked on the doorsteps of their straw-thatched mud houses. Sometimes we would cut through the birches, leaving the safety of the black tarmac road with it's aggressive yellow centre lines, and plunge onto a potholed track. We would skitter over the fields until some factory-like building would loom up, and a couple of passengers would leave our merry little crew. The snoggers finally left me to enjoy the back seat on my own at a factory that seemed to be producing straw mats. Lines of mats extended into the far distance in every direction, and still more were being humped around by wiry young men. Maybe they were for thatching, but I didn't have anyone to ask.

And at last we got to Zhalong itself. Not the nature reserve; the village. It was all mud huts and piles of hay. It seemed rather a sweet place. A tubby young girl rushed up to meet her father off the bus. He was laden with sweets from town and showered her in presents. But I could see no sign of the marshes. I now had to negotiate with the driver to take me on to see the birds. I didn't know the word for 'bird,' so was reduced to humiliating displays of arm-flapping-animal-imitation before he would admit to understanding me. I was tired, and agreed limply to his first offer of 50 kuai – far too much I am sure, especially considering I had only paid 8 kuai so far from Qiqihaer. But he was offering to wait for me and then drive me back. I wasn't sure of the bus situation to get back, and with the first flush of my intrepidness starting to ebb away, I was happy to have a certain lift back.

Low as my expectations were, I was disappointed by the reserve. A motley collection of shabby concrete buildings nestled around a collection of cages that were filled well beyond capacity with some miserable, squawking birds. The fact that surrounding this tourist area, there was this enormous wilderness of marshland inhabited by thousands of the wild birds couldn't have been less relevant. It was just a more inconvenient version of the cage at the zoo. I wandered around the cages for a while, watching my driver prod the birds with a stick in an effort to make them perform for me in some way. But hilarious though this undoubtedly was, I eventually tired of it after a few seconds and wandered off down a path that I hoped would lead to more of a wilderness area. Sure enough, once out of the direct environs of the tourist attraction, the marshlands are quite beautiful in a bleak way. There were very few birds, and I had forgotten my 25km telescope, so I was unable to see any of the actually wild cranes. But being as close to the camp as I still was, there were still a few of the tame birds that hang around to get fed. These occasionally took a break from their main pastime of standing on one leg in order to jump into the air and soar about for a bit, which made a graceful spectacle against the setting sun. The air was clean and there was a faint scent (a scent that I often pick up in wilderness places, and one that brings with it a very reassuring feeling) of Scotland. As I turned to head back to the camp, I noticed an anoraked man wearing an enormous camera chasing a bird around a small island. I remembered a sign that I had seen on the way in that sternly warned, "crane may attack person!" and once again found myself rooting for nature to bite back. Alas, the cowardly creature did not rise to the occasion, and timidly flapped its way to the other side of a patch of water before getting back to relaxing on one leg, it's head crammed in beneath its wing. It was time for me to head back home.

When we left the reserve my driver tried to re-negotiate for a higher price, claiming that he had had to wait too long for me. I knew at once what had brought this on: in a fit of louche laziness, I had not haggled enough over the price quoted to me in the gift shop. And we had had a short discussion about the exchange rate with England and I had shown everyone a twenty pound note (this always caused fascination). So now he thought that I was a money machine and would pay anything, and that he had aimed too low with fifty kuai. To my surprise, I now became quite stubborn, and refused to budge.

He tried some very low tricks, such as whining "I thought we were friends," before starting on a stunningly annoying line of "I'm only asking for one pound more – that's nothing to you." To his dismay, I remained firm. And returned to gazing out of the window.

"Here," the driver piped up as we entered a decrepit little settlement, "there are now no people."

"Really?" I replied, half-interested, and anyway glad that he seemed to have got over the dispute about the price.

"Yes! (This in a slightly incredulous tone) no people! Usually there are ten!" I looked skeptically back out at the little town. I could see a few people now, probably not ten, but more than none, and I began to doubt the reliability of my guide. I pointed at them.

"There are some people," I said, "one, two, three…"

"Urrrgghhhe!" he said, in that "you bloody moron" way at which the Chinese are so accomplished, "there are no people in this bus! There are usually ten! So you pay more!"

"Damn," I thought, blushing once again at my stupidity, before diving again into the tedious "you knew that when you first told me the price" argument. Eventually I offered to pay him an extra ten kuai if he drove me all the way back to the University. He fell silent until we reached the bus terminal.

“Ok, fifty kuai then,” he said. “Just take the bus to the University; it’s only one kuai, ten is far too much to pay.” He seemed suddenly friendly again, now that he was resigned to getting no more than his original price.

Chapter 22

The second tourist attraction that the guidebook mentioned was an island in the river called Mingyue Dao. So the day after my visit to Zhalong, I decided to head down to the river and see if I could find a boat to take me over there.

I hadn't been down to the river since I had been ice swimming and with the passing of winter, it was unrecognisable. Instead of the bleak and dirty ice stretching into the distance, I found a shimmering expanse of clear water lapping against the sand. Couples rowed boats around in a way that reminded me of the photo from the tourist guide. In some places, families had driven their cars down to the riverbank and were happily tucking into picnics, whilst some tinny tunes blared out from their car stereos. It would have been an idyllic scene, but for the certain knowledge that they were going to leave each and every piece of rubbish exactly where it fell.

In another place, I came across the rotting carcass of a collie-like mongrel. A herd of goats nosed around it, but didn't seem very interested. I wondered if it had been their 'goat-dog,' and if they were secretly rather pleased to see the sticky end to which it had come. I thought about asking the old man on crutches who seemed to be the goat-herd, but he was staring at me in a way that was just slightly too mad, and I hurried silently on.

As it happened, I didn't actually speak to anyone while I walked by the river, so I never got around to asking any of boat owners if they would take me to Mingyue Dao. Most of the other people down there were either young couples, whom I did not want to interrupt, or old men flying kites. There was something serenely dignified about these old men; having lived through such a turbulent period of history, they seemed charmingly content to spend their twilight years holding onto a piece of string with a plastic dragon attached to the other end. But I didn't want to disturb them either, and besides, I was happy enough just enjoying a rare moment of being unhassled by other people: I wasn't about to go hassling people myself. So I put off my visit to the island until another day.

Chapter 23

One of the other hobbies that I had developed over my time in Qiqihaer was an interest in the ethnic minorities of Heilongjiang. One group used to make their clothes out of fish skins. And I found a photograph of a man from another lot in his national dress, holding a spoon in his mouth with an egg in it. But my favourite minority was the Oroqen. They may not have been quite as weird as some of the others were, but they had a wild and romantic image that appealed to me. Prior to 'liberation' by the communists, they were a group of loosely affiliated clans that hunted over an enormous area spanning from 45 to 55 degrees of latitude and 115 to about 130 degrees of longitude; an area larger than Spain had been entirely theirs. I longed to visit them; to find out what had become of them since "liberation." I began by reading everything I could get my hands on about their history, and then started to try to track them down.

There had been about four thousand Oroqen, according to early twentieth century estimates; although it seems likely that there were once more, due to the numbers of them that were conscripted for military service in the Qing dynasty. Aside from military service, the Qing dynasty largely left them alone to continue their nomadic hunting lifestyle. The twentieth century was when things started to get bad for them. First the Japanese gave them a rough time when they took control of the region. They wanted to make use of the Oroqen's knowledge of the area and skills as hunters. So they strictly controlled all guns and ammunition, and forced the Oroqen to hand over everything that they killed to the Manchurian Animal Products Company, set up for the purpose. In return they were given such paltry rations that many starved to death, or died of exposure. The Japanese also distributed opium to the adult Oroqen in order to exercise further control over them. They were then forced into battle against the Chinese Communist Party's 'anti-Japanese army.'

After the Japanese had been defeated, Chiang Kai Shek forced the Oroqen to fight against the Communists once again. Memories of these anti-Communist roles would later make the Cultural Revolution especially difficult for the Oroqen; they were constantly humiliated and beaten, and many committed suicide. Shamans, clan leaders and other important people were tortured.

Once the Communists had taken control of the country, they encouraged the Oroqen to settle into towns. This was ostensibly because they were worried about the lack of food left in the forests. Though it might also have been that they wanted to chop down all of the forests for timber, and mine the hills for gold and other minerals, which they then proceeded to do. A combination of forest fires, aggressive logging and merciless poaching has left precious little in the way of wild life in these mountains.

On top of the wars, starvation and the destruction of the forests (and thus the animal population), huge quantities of mercury were used to float off non-gold debris in the gold mining processes that were now being carried out in the mountains, with unsurprising effects on the health of everyone living anywhere near. The Oroqen population took a dive and by the time they stopped being nomadic in about 1953, there were about 2000 of them left. But the area that many of them lived in was still, if only nominally, their own "Autonomous Banner." In 1951, the population in this area was 778 (774 Oroqen, 1 Ewenki, and 3 Daur.) By 1988, the immigration of Han Chinese had taken the population to 276,372, but with still about the same number of Oroqen as in 1951. Oddly it is still called the Oroqen Autonomous Banner, in spite of Oroqens accounting for less than 1% of the population. As an aside, it is quite strange that they were given an Autonomous Banner at all, and recognised as an ethnic minority; they themselves had no concept of their being a race until the communists settled them into towns and called them "Oroqen."

But now the government has changed its tune on Minorities, and they are treated well. They are not subject to the single child policy, and they get good handouts from the state. Their children are given relaxed entry requirements to state schools. All of this is serving to assimilate them still more quickly into the Han Chinese way of life.

Because they were so recently totally nomadic and cut off from the rest of the world, there are still some Oroqen alive today who were bought up in 'the old days.' I longed to meet these people and to hear tales of their lives, when they roamed over an area larger than Spain and hunted deer from horseback. But it seemed that I would need an introduction in order to meet them: their villages were remote, and difficult to find. Unless my Chinese improved dramatically, I would have no chance of finding them on my own.

I don't really know why, but I agreed to have lunch with Ardis again, to help her with her English. The first meeting had been torture, and normally it would have been the work of a moment for me to claim that I was 'too busy' and resolve never to answer the telephone to her again. But she caught me in a generous mood, and I said "Yes."

The meal started predictably badly; she was monosyllabic, and often didn't seem to understand me. To my astonishment, she suddenly became talkative at my mention of the Oroqen. Her parents were both brought up in a small village in the Greater Hinggan mountains, and only left when Ardis was about six years old, in order to go to the city where she would have better opportunities. Her uncle and aunt and her grandmother still live in the village, and had been badgering her to visit them before she went to England. As a temptation her uncle had said that he would take her to visit an Oroqen village. Ardis was not immensely keen on the idea but said that if I was, then she could arrange it and I could come with her. It was exactly the introduction that I needed. However, in Qiqihaer it was still barely spring, and the village was seventeen hours by train to the north. Up there it was still winter, and it would be too difficult to arrange anything while it was still cold; they don't like to do much other than drink baijiu in the winter. So we would wait until June, and meanwhile I would continue to teach Ardis by way of thanks for arranging the trip.

Chapter 24

Another project that had occupied much of my time was trying to find a place to shoot pheasants. Pheasants are native to Heilongjiang, so I felt confident that it must be possible to hunt them there. I scoured the internet, and had found an old web site referring to a hunting ground called Yuquan. Annoyingly, the site did not give the name in Chinese characters, so it was impossible to find it on a map, or to find the telephone number from directory inquiries. The web site said that Yuquan was sixty kilometres west of Harbin, so we scoured the map for places around that area that might be Yuquan. We found nothing. I tried asking just about everyone I knew if they knew anything about hunting, but none did. I tried getting Mr Guo to help me, but he either couldn't or just didn't want to. I was on the point of giving up when at last a total stranger on a bus said that he had heard of Yuquan. He wrote the characters down for me, and suddenly it was obvious: the name meant 'jade spring.' Now that I had the characters, I asked Joseph to call up directory inquiries.

Finally, after two months of searching, I called up the hunting ground to book myself in. I was going to meet Sam, a friend who was living in Hong Kong, in Harbin the next weekend, and since he was as keen on shooting as I was, I decided that we should go together. They took my booking, but confused me slightly by asking if we wanted to shoot donkeys as well as pheasants. This seemed to be a trifle unsporting, but I assured myself that I had probably misunderstood, and focused on the fact that they had definitely said that we could shoot pheasant.

As I took the train South, it seemed that I was travelling into spring. The grass became green, and the blossoms came out on the trees by the side of the tracks. I have never been made so aware of the passing of the seasons as I was on that journey.

I met up with Sam and took him to the grotty hotel that I had stayed in on my last visit to Harbin. We set off early the next morning in driving rain in yet another staunch little Volkswagon Santana. The rain did little to dampen our spirits; the name 'Jade Spring' had conjured up in our optimistic minds images of a paradise that even this downpour couldn't sour. Besides, we had waterproof jackets and a large hip flask of sloe vodka. Nothing could possibly go wrong.

As we approached Yuquan, the lush mountains rose up, and the road became steadily worse and worse. It was more pothole than tarmac, and we were reduced to walking pace. The tension mounted and mounted, and then we got lost. I was already impatient to arrive, and now I started to lose my temper with our driver. He seemed to find the situation completely hilarious, and offered no apology. I couldn't face the thought that, after all of this effort, my dream would be shattered because we would arrive too late and discover that the hunting parties all leave at nine o'clock in the morning, or some other disaster. I didn't want to miss out on this dream just because our driver was an incompetent fool.

Just as I was about to explode, a billboard on the right announced our arrival, and my doubts evaporated in a warm haze of realisation that we were actually finally *there*. We were actually going to hunt pheasant in their native mountains.

The long winding drive took us down a wooded valley in between rolling hills. At the end of the drive, we found the hunting lodge; a small hut painted in camouflage green, with a 'kang' inside as the heating system. We were each given a sturdy gun, and photographed outside in an excited pose. Then we set off into the woods with our guide – who, rather strangely, was wearing purple urban camouflage. After five minutes, we reached a tall fence that we were led through and then told to load up.

I spotted a pheasant at once. But the guide seemed to be deliberately ignoring it, and besides, there was now another man approaching us from the direction of the bird. I didn't want to shoot towards him, so although I was keen, I decided to sit tight and see what happened. The man who was approaching turned out to be the keeper. He asked us if we knew how to use the guns, and then told us to follow him. After walking for a further three metres, he 'spotted' the pheasant that I had seen before, and yelled furiously. Then he urgently crouched down in a rather misplaced and tardy effort at subtlety. The most surprising point, however, was that the pheasant itself was totally unmoved by any of this. It stood obliviously pecking away. It became clear that I was expected to shoot the poor beast as it pecked, but the British sporting sprit runs strongly in my veins and so I decided to chase it around and try to get it to fly. At first I crept up on it slowly, but it seemed unflustered by my presence. It just wandered slowly away from me, pecking as it went. At last I put down my gun and decided to run at it, hoping to drive it over Sam's head. To the keeper's obvious bemusement, and the pheasant's mild irritation, I scampered nimbly around in a circle three or four times, clapping my hands and making the "ayayayaaaaaayyy!" noises that one makes (for some reason) at pheasants. But I had no luck. The bird just beetled away up the hill and out of my reach.

"It can't fly," said the keeper at last.

"What? It a pheasant, isn't it? Pheasants can fly," I said.

"That one can't. But wait!" he said, rushing behind a tree and retrieving a big tarpaulin sack. He plunged his hand into the sack and pulled out another mangy bird, its feathers falling out and its neck bleeding in places. He wound himself up and hurled the poor creature as high as he could. It flew in a neat arc up to about thirty feet, when it finally spread its clipped wings and spluttered quickly down to earth.

"Shoot! Shoot!" shouted the keeper.

"Bloody hell" said Sam. I am not sure if the fall itself had killed the bird, or if it just couldn't be bothered to move when it had landed, but it lay completely still. We looked at each other, and considered whether we should just give up and go home.

But at this moment, Sam spotted a pigeon on the branch of a tree just behind us. We jumped with excitement, and decided to stalk it. Pigeons are notoriously jumpy customers, and will normally fly off long before you get close enough to shoot them. So we hunched down low and trod daintily. I moved around one side, while Sam crept around the other. We inched closer and closer, our hearts racing, our eyes fixed on the bird, waiting for it to make its move. At last we were almost standing beneath it, and I decided to make a noise to get it to fly. "Ayayayay!" I yelped, and the bird made his break. He leapt from the branch, our guns went up, and… and flapping his wings frantically, the pigeon spiralled to the ground like a sycamore seed. It was another set up with a flightless bird.

I can't quite understand how or why, but I still had some traces of enthusiasm left. Maybe it was the last vestiges of my dream of shooting in Heilongjiang that were refusing quite to die. Or maybe it was just a stubborn desire to "teach the bloody locals how to do it." Either way, I managed to persuade the keeper to take us up into the mountains in search of some wild birds. He told me that there were really very few birds up the mountain, and that anyway, it was an incredibly long walk. But that is the sort of shooting I wanted: a good long walk in the mountains with, maybe, a couple of brace of pheasants to show for it at the end. So off we went.

After about twenty minutes, the keeper announced that we had arrived. This threw me a little, because I thought that we were going to be wandering around the hills rather than going on a journey to a specific place. Besides we had only just started walking, and hadn't got above the plastic bag line yet. But he insisted that I load up, and instructed me to follow him closely. A moment later he pulled out a towel, and started to flap it wildly at a nearby tree stump. I craned my neck to get a closer look, just in time to see a hen pheasant being forced off her nest. She flapped a couple of times, and glided into a nearby thicket. The keeper made after her, cursing me for not shooting her before, but by now I had totally lost interest, and was pissed off with myself for not having realised that the shooting season in China would of course be the same as in England, in spite of their insistent claims that "there is no 'shooting season' in China."

Chapter 25

By the time I arrived back in Qiqihaer, the spring had truly arrived there too. Flowers were blooming, and there was a lively scent in the air. Couples walked hand in hand in the park and rowed on the lake. It seemed that it might one day become something other that the bleak grey city that I had known.

I didn't have time to get used to it though; I had an evening train to catch up to Inner Mongolia with Stefan. This was going to be a true adventure; I had longed to head off into the unknown armed only with a map. I still didn't have the confidence in my language skills to do it totally alone though, and since Stefan had expressed an interest in the mountains, and since he spoke far better Chinese than I did, we decided to go together. No guidebook mentioned this enormous area at all so we had no plans, except a general idea that we would find some interesting people and places.

Stefan sat on his bunk on the train and studied. I was too excited to study, and stared out of the window at the unchanging scenery until it got dark. Then I made myself some pot noodles. I ended up pouring hot water all over the bed on the bottom bunk. The rather sinister engineer whose bed it was had gone off to the loo, so I had a few minutes to try to cover up my blunder. I busied around trying to dry it with various tools, and ending up making the stain quite a lot worse. Finally I decided to sit on it, in the hope that I could cover the stain up for long enough for my trousers to soak it up. Soon, too soon, the engineer returned. I had to rudely not allow him to sit on his own bed. I stared out of the window and pretended not to notice him. He was very insistent though, and started shouting at me to get up, and shaking me roughly. When I finally relented, and stood shakily up, a cloud of steam rose from the stain on the bed and from my crotch: my trousers had had time to soak up just enough of the water so that there was a dark wet patch both on my trousers and the bed. This explained (as far as the sinister engineer was concerned) why I was so reluctant to move from his bed. I had clearly wet myself while sitting on his bed. There was a moment of stunned silence while everyone in the compartment took in this disturbing development, and then the engineer began to shout. He shouted and shouted, and thrashed his arms in anger. But he didn't really know quite what else to do. I looked at my shoes and shuffled a lot and hoped that a solution would present itself. Eventually, during a pause in the shouting, I offered to let him have my bed. Much to my surprise he did not agree, but seemed to consider this still more offensive and started shouting with renewed vigour. By the time he had finished I was feeling so guilty that I had almost forgotten that I had only, in fact, spilled water on his bed. But eventually he calmed down, or ran out of energy, and allowed me to slink red-faced up to my top-bunk hideaway, where I tried to get some sleep.

I woke early, as I always do on trains. Outside there was snow on the ground, and a spating river wound through the birch forest in a way that made me itch for my fishing rod. I sat and stared vacantly out at it for the last hour of the journey, dreaming of the adventures we might have. At last the stout, new, brightly painted buildings of Yi Tu Li He loomed out of the forest. These were the central buildings; the station, a couple of apartment blocks around the station and the single paved road that ran up the hill away from the station. The rest of the town consisted of wooden huts crammed together around allotment gardens. As we arrived, we were mobbed by hungry taxi drivers wanting to charge us enormous prices to take us to see 'fascinating' sights. Had I been on my own, I may have, in a moment of weakness, given in to these demands; and later regretted it. As it was, we held firm as a team, and refused to discuss anything with anyone until after breakfast. While we ate a reassuringly tasteless breakfast (good food would have made us feel that we were not being adventurous enough), we poured over the map and discussed where we should head. Most of the smaller towns seemed to have names that suggested a role in forestry. This, we thought, wouldn't be that interesting. And probably would make them very hard to get to. So we decided instead to see where we could get a bus to, and then get that bus.

"You've come too early; it's ugly here now," said the man on the next door table, being only the first in a long line of people that we would meet who were insistently pessimistic about the area. I hadn't noticed this trait in China before; even in Qiqihaer, the possessor of perhaps the most uninteresting scenery in the entire world, people managed to constantly tell me how beautiful the city's setting is.

"Where can we take a bus to from here?" Stefan asked, hoping for some useful tips.

"There's nowhere really worth going to. You want to go to Qiqihaer; that's a nice, big city. Lots to do."

"We have come from there, we have seen big cities. We want to see some smaller places."

"That's boring." They didn't seem to get the point. We decided to go and climb up the hill opposite the town and to think some more about where to go after lunch. As we left the restaurant, there was an enormous billboard showing a happy family (only one child), and behind them some wonderful new sky scrapers. "Practice family planning for a happy and prosperous society" read the text. The contrast between the skyscrapers in the picture and the decrepit huts that stood all around us seemed to suggest that some of the locals had been doing a little bit too much breeding.

We met a Mongolian man in a small local shop. He leapt off his horse just outside, and tethered it to a tree. It reminded me of a scene from a Western. We walked with him towards the hill, and he showed us the best route up. He said that he liked to climb up the hills on weekends as well. He was the first person in China that I had met who had shown anything other than a total lack of understanding that anyone could possibly enjoy climbing mountains. And I felt a real warmth towards him because of it. He worked in forestry (as we were to find out, almost everyone there who had a job worked in forestry); he cut down trees and then used his horse to drag them out of the forest. It seems a very primitive way to do it, but then maybe it is the cheapest.

The hill was cloaked in a forest of the brilliant silver birches that cover most of this area. It was still and beautiful in a way that I had almost forgotten that things could be. The only sounds were the birds in the trees and the distant whistle of a train in the valley. This was a very welcome change from the rest of China. We saw what I am sure was a chipmunk, and spent a while stalking it to take some photographs that would be totally uninteresting to look at later. Coming back down the hill, we went a different way and ended up in deep snow scrambling down a very steep face. It was fun though, and I felt happily remote for a short while.

Coming back into the town we chatted to a bunch of toothless old ladies who were sitting on a bench.

"There was a foreigner here last year as well," one observed.

"Yes," said another, "he climbed that mountain too." How very predictable we foreigners are. Over the next few hours many people asked us if we had climbed the hill yet. I never quite worked out whether this was the result of an astonishing rumour mill that had spread the news of our intentions so fast, or if it was simply that every foreigner likes to climb these hills. Either way, they evidently found our love for hills as confusing as we found their indifference.

"We live with the mountains, so they do not interest us," one man told us. I don't know how Stefan resisted from telling him that in Austria he lived with mountains that would dwarf these, but was still interested by them. Except for that one Mongolian man, we just have different attitudes, and they are mutually unintelligible.

We ended up eating lunch at the same restaurant as we had had breakfast, after being led on a roundabout route via another hotel, by a young girl who was sent by her mother to guide us. It was a small town, so it was no surprise that we should be taken to the same restaurant twice. But it was gratifying to go back there and say our "hellos" like old friends. We felt like we belonged. In this mood of good humour towards the locals, we decided to ask for some local specialties for lunch. Looking back, this seems to me to be a staggeringly stupid and risky thing to have done, and so it proved to be. They served up the one thing (well, not the *one*, but one of the very few things) that I truly cannot eat: pig's trotters. But they were served with such pride and happiness that it was clear that I was going to have to stop being pathetic about it and get stuck in. I confidently seized a hoof in my hand and tried to believe that I was going to enjoy it, as I greedily chomped at the greasy orange fat around the tendons. Positive mental attitude is a large part of the game when trying to eat revolting foods, but alas, it is not the whole game. These trotters were the most pungently disgusting thing that I have ever tried to eat. I've eaten maggots, grubs and eyeballs. I've eaten most disgusting sounding things that I have ever come across. But once again the pig's trotter stumped me. They taste exactly like a pig smells; they taste like pig shit. That isn't surprising, given that your average pig's trotter spends most of its life trotting in pig shit. I spluttered and spat it out. I burned my tongue on my tea as I tried to take to taste away. It was time to leave town.

We headed north to the village of Hao Li Pu, a similar place to Yi Tu Li He but without the new buildings. This was just a collection of wooden huts. As we strolled around, marvelling at the amount of 'single child policy' propaganda, we collected a hoard of children around us. Some chatted to us and pointed out sights of marginal interest, while others ran ahead alerting their friends to our presence with cries of "Waiguoren! Waiguoren!" I liked the children; they alone did not feel compelled to ask us why we had come to such a crappy place, or to tell us that we should go on to Gen He (the local big city). They led us down the muddy streets lined with tall scruffy wooden fences. Intermittently, proud little porches would break up the fences, opening into messy private yards filled with pigs and tiny raggedly ploughed fields. By the river, a man washed his fake Honda motorcycle while a cowherd trundled past with his cows.

I spent the day being the moronic giant as I struggled to keep up with the questions that Stefan put to them. His Chinese was very good, and once people got used to speaking to him, they started to ask me questions that were well beyond my ability. It was rather depressing, but it was a true reflection of how far I still had to go, and it did make me glad that I hadn't come alone.

At one point a savage looking and rather mangy dog leapt out from a side alley and barked and bared its teeth ferociously. I reached for a stick with which to fend it off but before I had need of it, the dog rushed off and struggled through a tiny gap in a fence. It then continued to shout its savage threats from the safety of its fortress. It seemed a thoroughly intelligent and altogether undog-like thing to have done. I liked the dog for it, diseased though it probably was.

The village had seen better days. The cinema now had shrubs growing out of the dripping roof, and it had not been used for years. In every town that we went to there was a cinema or a 'culture hall' that had fallen into total disrepair. There used to be a thriving market here, so the children told us. But now there were just a few stalls left; most people went to the big stores in Gen He, so the market just couldn't survive. There was also no running water in any of the towns that we went to. "China is developing so fast," everyone says. But not up here. There are fewer and fewer jobs, and people are poor. But they didn't seem unhappy about it.

The oldest of the children – he must have been about seventeen – found us a horrid little guesthouse with pungently smelly beds and a pile of shit in the corner of the yard that functioned as the loo, and we decided to stay. He told us that he knew a place where there were about 100 Ewenki living in the mountains. He suggested that he would take us there in the morning. We carefully took down his number, and went to bed full of excitement. But when we called the next day, the person that picked up told us that we had got the wrong number. He knew the guy that we were asking for, but said that this was not the right number to call on. The answer was simple: he didn't really want to take us there; he was just being polite in offering. That is often the way: if they really want to do something for you, then they will call you. Don't call them. But it was very disappointing nonetheless.

As we travelled around the other towns in the area, we chatted with the locals, and learned a bit about what went on there. The only real industry was forestry. These towns were all built about fifty years ago to service the forestry industry. The boom years are over now though, and jobs are being lost. Those who don't actually chop down trees seem to be involved in fire prevention. They have big fires every year. And yet they do not seem to use fire breaks at all. None of them seemed to understand the concept. Maybe there is a good reason for that, or maybe the companies just don't want to lose an area that could be used for growing trees.

We learned even more about the general Chinese habits of conversation. Stefan shares my distaste for small talk. He would rather just sit in silence than ask a pointless question. But the Chinese are such consummate experts at the game that it didn't seem to matter. "Austria, Austria," they'd repeat for full minutes after Stefan had answered the "where are you from" question, just to avoid a silence. They will also repeat the same question almost ad infinitum just to fill time.

"Ah! Drinking tea!" said one man as he came into our little room at a restaurant and sat himself down. He seemed to think that that was a good enough opening gambit. After a few minutes of silence he went on “not drinking alcohol?”

“No.”

“Just come here to eat and drink tea, eh?” he sounded slightly confused. This is another Dongbei concept: a restaurant is not primarily a place to eat; it is primarily a place to brink baijiu. It is only because you need to eat something to take that foul taste away that these people eat at all. That is probably why there are no bars in these small towns. There is just no call for them.

While we were having dinner in this small northern town, we foolishly gave in to this local custom and called for a bottle of baijiu. This wasn’t just mindless bravado; we wanted to drink something, but we decided that beer was too dangerous because it would lead to a need to go to the loo in the night, which would mean taking on the pile of shit in the yard in the dark. That was just too terrible to contemplate. So we really had no choice but to take the hard road and go for baijiu. The sight of two foreigners drinking baijiu proved to be too much of an encouragement to the charming restaurateur, who took it as the green light to come and join us for several more bottles. The concept of drinking ‘just a bit’ is not one with which they are familiar. He was thrilled to have two foreigners with him, and we had our pictures taken with the whole family. They showed us around town, which was small and pitch dark at night, except for the lights of the two karaoke bars. So we went to both. We ate some more food. They gave us chicken heads on a stick, and we crunched their heads and sucked out their brains, too drunk to care. We swore that we would return when the spring had come and that we would go fishing in the mountains, and we parted friends. They hadn’t tried to show us any tourist sights. They hadn’t tried to rip us off for anything; in fact they had bought us a lot of food and a lot to drink. They had just been incredibly kind to us from beginning to end. I liked these people.

When we got back to Yi Tu Li He, a young boy clutching a black kitten rushed up to us and asked "are you Chinese or are you Foreigners?" He was the second child to ask us that sort of question. It's strange that they don't know what we look like; they may be poor, but they all have television.

As we waited for our train home, I reflected on how tiny this station had seemed when we had arrived just three days before, and yet how big and advanced it now looked. We had become remarkably used to the mountain life remarkably quickly. It is quiet, and it is not glamorous. In an odd sort of a way, I started to be able to actually feel the excitement of going to the big city, and, even more oddly, I began to feel that excitement about going to Qiqihaer. I don't think that I will ever have the Chinese love for crowds or for concrete cities. I will always prefer the mountains and the wilderness. But having this feeling of heading up to the big city, and looking forward to the bright lights, I did at least feel that I could empathise with them to a small extent.

Chapter 26

During the winter months, the students were put to work in the mornings, breaking up the ice on the roads. They worked in gangs, one gang swinging pitchforks to smash the ice, while the next one shovelled it up into a pile on the pavement. Later, as the ground thawed, I saw hundreds of them at work digging holes in every area of grass on the campus. Trees were then dropped into these as a part of the University's involvement in 'National Tree Planting Day.' I had never really worked out what I thought of this forced labour: was it good training, and an economical way of getting these jobs done, or was it an infringement of the students' rights?

These doubts were confused still further when I went to throw my rubbish out of the window one morning, to find the campus thronging with students picking up stray rubbish and returning it to the tip. The attitude of the Chinese to rubbish had long rankled with me. They discard everything the very moment that they decide that they no longer have use for it; wherever they may be at the time. Later in the summer I unwrapped an ice cream and was just going to put the wrapper in the bin, when a frantic old man interrupted me.

"Blah blah blah foreigner blah blah blah!" he shouted, and I assumed from his tone that he was being offensive.

"Excuse me, I just want to put this in there," I said, pointing at the bin.

"I know, I know," he said in a quieter and more comprehensible voice. "That is what I am saying: you foreigners use the bin for rubbish. We Chinese just throw it where we stand; this is why

China is full of rubbish. It is bad. Thank you," he shook my hand and disappeared off into the crowd.

So seeing these students being forced to pick up rubbish did make me happy. It was totally ineffective from the point of view of keeping the campus clean; as soon as the next breeze blew, all of the rubbish was whipped out of the tip and spread out across the campus again. But I was happy because someone, somewhere in the university, had recognised that there was too much rubbish around. And maybe, just maybe, if the students are made to pick up rubbish enough, then they will start putting it in bins to begin with.

Chapter 27

Qiqihaer Buddhist monastery is a confusing place. A sign at the entrance tells us that it has "as many as sixty years of history," which sounds amazingly recent for a monastery. Apparently a monk from Southern China had come up to Qiqihaer in 1939 to set it up because there was only one other Buddhist monastery in the whole of Dongbei. It had only just been finished when the Cultural Revolution came along and it was burned to the ground. Just three years after Chairman Mao had died and the Cultural Revoloution had ended, the rebuilding of the monastery began. In 1987, after seven years of rebuilding, it was listed as a "cultural artifact to be protected by Heilongjiang province." This was just fifteen years after Heilongjiang province had decided that it was a cultural artifact and so must be destroyed, but such was the lunacy of the Cultural Revolution.

The rebuilding is still in progress; the monastery is spread over 32 hectares, and there is much to be done. I went to see it with Manfred, who had just got back from Tibet and was unimpressed by their efforts.

"The painting is awful. The colours are too bright. It looks like a child's painting, not a monastery," he said, and to an extent I agreed. The roves *were* too bright a shade of yellow, and the painting on the beams *was* crass and indelicate. But that didn't really bother me. I liked the fact that they were making the effort to rebuild it at all. And it wasn't just as a tourist attraction; in fact the tourist guide doesn't even mention it as a place to visit.

It is being put back together as a functioning Buddhist monastery. Monks in pale yellow robes pottered around wearing far-away expressions. Businessmen burned incense sticks, and prayed for success. Students, who were worried about their exams, came to ask for good results. All of these were dressed in the ubiquitous Western clothes, but they are indubitably going about *Chinese* lives. Their clothes aside, there was no hint of Westernisation. The buildings may not be as beautiful as those in Tibet, but where in the world can afford or is able to put up buildings with the same level of intricate carving and detailed decoration that was possible in past times?

It seemed to me at the time that this was a very inspiring message. I wrote in my journal that "they are doing it because they are Buddhists, and want to have their temple back… it shows that the Chinese culture has managed to survive the purges of the 70s, and so it fills me with optimism." But looking back, I think that I may have been too easily persuaded. The businessmen who came to pray for success were probably not really practicing Buddhists. There are relatively few of them left. Many of the students that I spoke to were unable to tell me the differences between Daoism and Buddhism. They seemed to go to the temple more for superstitious than for religious reasons.

The government likes to sponsor the rebuilding of these religious sites in order to show that the insanity of the Cultural Revolution is over. But rebuilding the temples does not bring back the knowledge and tradition that was destroyed. It seems they have built a temple where people can go to focus on their superstitions, but nothing more.

It was a confusing place, and not especially beautiful. But few beautiful places have ever interested me as much.

Chapter 28

Jim once said to me that he felt that he found living in Qiqihaer possible only because we lived in that foreigners' dormitory, and China stopped at the front door. The chaos and bustle and spitting and shouting were made tolerable by the fact that we could retreat into our concrete safe house, and no one could touch us. Instinctively I didn't like this idea. It seemed to me that we were here precisely to experience the hustle and bustle of Chinese life, and that it was a great pity that we had to leave that world every time we went home.

These rather pious views were put to the test when the rule forbidding Chinese people to enter our dormitory was waived for a large group of sports students. About thirty of them arrived one afternoon and stayed for two weeks to take a scholarship to study Sport at the University. At first I relished the opportunity to speak Chinese to people in my neighbouring rooms.

"Soon," I thought, "I will have thirty or so Chinese friends right here in my own building. What could be better?"

The Americans took a different view and started locking the kitchen to stop the Chinese from raiding our food and stealing our frying pans. I chuckled at their paranoia, and started trying to make friends with the new arrivals.

I used to smile and say "ni hao!" in a jovial tone whenever I saw one of them. They always looked frightened if they were on their own, and ran away. If they were in a group, they looked at each other and laughed loudly. I laughed too in the hope that this would endear me in some way. But it never did.

They were always up extraordinarily early, rushing up and down the corridors practicing triple jump or out in the yard throwing the shot put or some other athletic training. They always made a lot of noise.

Two days after their arrival, our hot water was turned off completely, robbing us of even the dream of a hot early morning shower. The reason given for this was that now there were so many people in the dormitory, they could not afford to give us all hot water. So they gave us none. The popularity of the sports students amongst the others in the dormitory fell still further. It didn't affect my life though, because I had long since given up trying to catch the fleeting minutes of hot water, and always took cold showers. What really got to me was the spitting.

When I wanted to get some hot water for my tea, I was accustomed to making the short trip down to the kitchen without putting on my shoes. The floor is cleaned every morning, and I didn't think that it could really get *that* dirty over the course of a single day. How wrong I was.

I had just started off down the corridor with my Nescafe jar, when a shouting group of sweaty students dressed in skimpy 'wife-beaters' burst out of one of the rooms, and rushed past me, spitting furiously as they went. As the dust settled on the empty corridor, the faux-marble floor glistened with pools of saliva and phlegm. I had a hard enough time picking my way back the three metres to my room, and certainly wasn't brave enough to take on the next twenty metres without the back up of my shoes. Now I understood what Jim meant about the unwelcome invasion of China into our dormitory. I had to admit that I enjoyed my little cocoon of Westernisation as much as anyone else did.

Chapter 29

By the middle of May, summer really appeared to have come to Qiqihaer, and the locals had taken to dining outside. They took little barbecues and motley selections of chairs out onto the pavements and sat there 'ganbeiing' baijiu and hurling good-natured words at each other. The air was filled with the thick scent of burning charcoal, and if you lost concentration, you could find yourself feeling almost back at home at a summer barbecue. The incessant noise of the tinny announcements from the stadium where the sports trials were being held, interspersed with the occasional bout of scratchy big band music that signaled the approach of yet another race, soon shattered your day dream though.

In town, the streets bustled. It was as though the hoards of people who had been sucked inside, safe behind their airlocks for the bitter winter months, had been exhaled onto the pavements. Bicycle rickshaws wove to and fro in the alleys, and the zebra crossings were marching columns. The thick carpet flaps that hung over every entrance to keep out the cold had been taken down, and the shops spilled out into the open.

One afternoon, I set out from my safe little cocoon of Westernisation to buy an international phone card for my mobile. I wanted the 200 kuai one. The girl in the shop wanted me to pay fifty kuai for it. I had long since ceased to associate the *value* of a phone card with the price that should be paid for it, so I started to haggle. Eventually I got it for 40. This was more than I had paid the time before, but maybe prices had risen, or maybe I was just a gullible foreigner. Either way, after weeks of placid acceptance of this system of haggling for something that had a set price printed on it, it suddenly struck me as strange. How could they sell these cards for such a small fraction of their value?

It was the same with stamps: buy them at the post office, and you paid the price that is written on them. But buy them on the street, and you paid about 60% of that. Manfred once tried to do this in Beijing, but they just laughed at him.

“You can do it in Qiqihaer,” he said.

“That’s Qiqihaer, this is Beijing!” they laughed. I don’t know why Qiqihaer should be so different. It does have a reputation for being a city of thieves though, so maybe the thieves were stealing the cards and selling them at cut prices.

In the evenings, I used to go for long bike rides by the river. I loved it down there. I rode along the floodwall and gazed over the water. Silhouetted against the setting sun were little fishing boats with tiny canvas sails running back to the shore. The water was high, and all of what used to be the beach was underwater. Only the trees poked out, about half of their trunks above water. I don’t know if this was because of snow melting in the mountains, or if it was a result of the dam that they had put in while they built a bridge; there had been very little rain, and certainly nothing to warrant this flood. But the huge expanse of water gave the riverbank a ‘seaside’ feel. The ice cream vendors were usually packing up as I cycled past, and the peddle boats had been pulled back up the embankment. It was an evening sight from any seaside resort: a bit seedy, but that was part of the charm.

With the warm weather came a spate of weddings. When there was a big one, the whole city reverberated throughout the day to the sound of fireworks. I once saw a wedding going on between one Mr Wang and one Miss Zhang. I was rather pleased because at the time these were two of the four or so Chinese names that I could read, and I was thrilled to be able to understand the banner that flew over the entrance to the hotel where the reception was being held.

They had gone in for the most gratuitous display of wealth that I had yet seen in China. The front of the hotel was awash with rented Mercedes. All had even-numbered number plates, as is the custom at weddings. There was an enormous red inflatable arch decorated with balloons, underneath which several dancers dressed in traditional costumes leapt and rolled and pranced around each other. Pigeons poured out of a container in the corner in a constant stream lasting for about a minute, and a cannon began firing exploding shots into the air – a lucky number of shots that had been chosen by a wise old woman to suit the couple. Other fireworks started early that morning, and had continued ever since, loudly declaring the wealth of the happy couple. In the middle of this festival of Chinese customs and traditions stood the dinner-jacketed groom and his lovely bride; her veil was drawn back, her face was caked in make-up and a natty pair of bright red buckled shoes peeped out from beneath her enormous white meringue wedding dress.

Chapter 30

An irritating young lad took to lingering around the dormitory and trying to speak English with all of us. Hundreds of students did this over the months that I was in Qiqihaer, but this one was the most irritating and persistent. He first cornered Manfred and me as we sat on the front step enjoying the sunshine and taking occasional sips from my hip flask of Sloe Vodka.

"You-a-speak-a-English? You-a-like footaball? Daveee Beck-a-ham?" he started out, and at once we were looking for an escape. But although we tried our best to be off hand, he remained keen. Somehow he got the notion that we were getting on well, and he started to 'horse around' with me in the most thoroughly annoying way; he grabbed the hip flask and, while my mind was briefly elsewhere, he forced it into my mouth. He tipped my head backwards and howled with laughter; I was snapped out of my quiet thoughts with an angry jolt. He was much younger than me, and much smaller. It was all I could do to stop myself from becoming violent with him. God knows how, but I managed to limit myself to a stern look, before turning my back to him in a way that I hoped would let him know that I was really very pissed off, and struggling not to plant a fist on the end of his snub little nose. He read the situation differently. I had, in his view, turned my back in order to better allow him to lean over and whisper into my ear. As I felt his stinking warm breath oozing over my ear, it was only the urge to vomit that kept me from tearing him to pieces in a fit of anger and revulsion. But whilst I wretched, I heard what he was saying, and couldn't help laughing: "You a-makeee the *Luuurve*?" He had clearly heard, as all Chinese have, that Westerners are very direct, and so they think that these sort of questions are perfectly reasonable ones to put to perfect strangers. As I laughed, he finally started to look upset, as though finally I had managed to do something to offend him.

"Oh, No!" he whined, "my Eeenglerlish so bad!" I laughed again at this pathetic effort to excuse his boldness; was he going to try to pretend that he had wanted to ask my name or some other innocent question? But no, he continued: "I mean to say, "Do you FUCK?" " He shouted the last word, and I pathetically melted into derisive laughter, my anger suddenly abated, but I was feeling no kinder towards the boy.

"I don't understand; ask Heather, her English is better than mine," I said, and went inside.

I think that it was a great failing of mine that I could never learn to deal with this type of Chinese student. They are keen to practice their English, and I should have been able to respect them for that. But their manner of interaction was unbearable. They had an appallingly direct and intense way of talking to you. They would plant their face inches from yours and ask you if you masturbate or if you have seen a Chinese dick before. I knew that they wouldn't ask another Chinese person such absurd and direct questions; it is just that they have been told that Westerners are direct and have no morals, so they think that this is how we talk to each other. I probably shouldn't have blamed them for their irritating way of speaking, but I couldn't help it. I found it too annoying.

The culture difference often makes it difficult to make friends with the Chinese students; they had such very different interests and ambitions. Perhaps it was for this reason that the main bookstore started selling a book entitled 'How to Marry a Western Man.' This book tried to explain some of the cultural differences, and to help the young Chinese girl to say the right thing to keep her man interested. Because it was written for the Chinese, it was written in Chinese. Therefore I could not understand more than a tiny amount of it. However, it had some 'phrasebook' sections that were written in English, and these were pure dynamite. Here are some of my favourite extracts:

What you should say to your Western man:

"You're very strong – are you strong in everything you do?"

"Of course I like Western food"

"Yes, you do look good in that green and orange tie"

"Yes I do understand that joke – I think it's really funny"

"Why would I be different from your first/second/third/fourth wife?"

And here are some of the phrases that your Western man is most likely to say to you:

"My wife is being very difficult and will not give me a divorce"

"Of course it's not just about sex"

"All Western women do this in bed – you should too"

"I own my own business, I have two houses, three cars and a horse on my ranch"

"No, no, no – I don't like big breasts at all"

And the final, and, I imagine, the most irresistibly seductive of all:

"I love your culture, I love China – please come to bed"

We asked in the shop if the book was supposed to be funny, and we were told that it was not; it was a serious instruction manual.

Chapter 31

There was an email going around a while ago that showed a picture of a disgruntled woman holding a chicken McNugget that was in fact a chicken's head lightly coated in batter. She had been about to eat this tasty morsel, when her son intervened, screaming wildly, and she was saved. She sued McDonalds and, according to the email, got $100,000 in damages. I had first seen it back in England, and had vaguely thought "how repellent," before promptly forgetting about it. Then Stefan sent it to me just after we got back from Inner Mongolia, where we had eaten chicken's heads. I chuckled to myself at just how much my reaction to the photograph had changed. What had been horror at the repellent chicken's head was now amazement that a company should have to pay a customer $100,000 for giving them something that was entirely edible. It just seemed ridiculous. Then I promptly forgot about it once more.

However, Stefan also sent the email to Theo, who took it one stage further. He saw in this little cultural anomaly a chance for a good English lesson. He printed out the sheet and gave it to his students. Their English level was pretty high, at least their reading level was, and they should have had no trouble in understanding it. But when it came to finding out what they had understood from the article, it turned out that they thought that the woman had bought the chicken's head for $100,000. There is no way that you can get that impression from the text of the article; it was simply that they were so confounded by the thought that anyone could *not* want the chicken's head, and even more, be *paid* for having received one, that they refused to believe what they read. They warped it to mean something that they could believe; like a chicken's head costing $100,000. Far from being the anti-McDonalds story that it was posed as, this could actually be used as an advertising campaign in

China: “One in a hundred Chicken McNuggets will be a GENUINE chicken’s head!” would be a possible strap line. You’d have the Chinese flooding in.

Chapter 32

On those warm summer nights, we often sat out on the pavement drinking beer with Guang Fong, the shop owner from across the road. We perched on a motley collection of plastic stools clustered around a dim light bulb that dangled from a washing line. The rest of the street was dark and empty except for the occasional taxi that would stop and beep its horn, hoping to persuade us that we wanted to go somewhere. Guang Fong was one of my first and certainly one of my best Chinese friends. He was from Qiqihaer, but he moved down to Shenzhen in Southern China for a few years in his early twenties, where he met his wife. When they got married, he looked at his wife's birth certificate, and discovered that she was not, as she had claimed, the same age as him, but in fact was five years older. She still insists that he would not have married her if he had known her true age earlier on. Then they came back up here together (quite why she had made such efforts at deception in order to marry someone who would make her move to Qiqihaer is not clear) and started a little stall selling snacks by the University. That was eight years ago. Slowly they built up enough cash to move out of the gaggle of street vendors, and to start their own shop. He says that he earns 100 kuai (about £7) a day from the shop. But he also owns a flat where his parents live, and another flat where he and his family live if ever they don't stay at the shop (which is rarely). So he must be getting the cash in somewhere.

One of the Russians once asked him (for some difficult to fathom reason) if he could get hold of an AK-47 for him. He seemed to think that it would be possible. On the strength of this and other similar comments, we inferred that he must have some 'contacts.' I think that this may be a prerequisite to doing any business in Qiqihaer; there are 'tax' collectors who come round and look at the shop a couple of times a year, and according to how much they like you/how much you bribe them, they ask you to pay up a certain amount. All tax collection in China seems to be done not by the government itself, but by tax collection companies. These companies pay a certain amount to the government, and keep the rest for themselves. Since they have the government behind them, they can make life extremely difficult for anyone who doesn't pay. It is like a ready-made Mafia, without even needing to bother being violent with the debtors. You can just shut them down. Since Guang Fong runs a shop, he must have had some contact with these people. And since he seemed to have done extremely well for himself in a very short period of time, we reckoned that he must have something dodgy going on with them. I don't know if we were right, and it could well just have been our fertile imaginations working overtime. But he was always very kind to me, even when I could barely say 'hello,' in Chinese, and getting to know him better was one of the great pleasures of starting to speak the language.

Chapter 33

Ever since the debacle over my art teachers staying up all night playing computer games, I had harboured a quiet fascination for the 'internet café' culture that seemed to abound in Qiqihaer.

"They just have nothing else to do," someone told me when I asked.

"It is so cheap for them, and allows them to escape from their mundane lives in Qiqihaer," said someone else. I can't quite remember how the idea emerged, but we were discussing the phenomenon one evening at supper, and before I knew it, I had agreed to go with Manfred and to find out for ourselves.

As dinner ended, I set off with Manfred (who knows how to work computer games, which I don't), a thermos of coffee, and several packs of cigarettes (we felt that cigarettes were probably essential to creating the correct, rather gritty, atmosphere) to find a twenty-four hour café. We tried the place opposite the dormitory, but found it disappointingly closed. Then we tried the other two nearby places. Both of these were also sternly locked with heavy chains. What had happened to the myth of the 24-hour gaming?

Finally, we got a taxi driver to take us across town to a dingy little back-street café where the lights were still on, and the door was unlocked. It was eleven fifteen, and I was quite tired.

The lights were low, and a scattering of eager gamers stared vacantly at their cyber-worlds, their faces flashing in the reflected light of the screen. Few people were talking, and the only sounds were the "aaarrrgh!'s" and gunfire and thudding of bullets into flesh that make up the music for most of these games. I won't say that I was excited at the prospect of becoming a part of this alien community, but I was at least genuinely interested. On the most idealistic level, I liked the idea that a whole bunch of us from all over the world could spend an evening playing games together, regardless of our race or language. We could rush around an imaginary world, sometimes shooting each other and sometimes working as a team. We could form a coalition of strangers from all corners of the globe, fighting in a pointless war in which no one got hurt. And that seemed to me to be rather a wonderful idea.

As is usual with me and computers, we spent the first hour or so trying to work out how to start the right program. We chose the enticingly named 'counter strike' as our first entertainment of the evening. We then spent another hour or so pissing around with passwords before finally we were allowed to enter the game. We decided that it would be more fun if we were on the same team, and chose the "anti-terrorist" squad. A couple of well placed 'clicks,' and we were in. I had to escort a VIP (Manfred) through a ruined castle to a 'safety zone,' avoiding the team of terrorists that would be trying to 'take us out' at every turn. Or at least that was the idea.

We hid back in a safe little corner for a while, whilst we got the hang of the controls. Then we timidly set out. At every corner I would dart out into the open and back again, peering around for any enemy. After repeating this a few times, once I was really sure that we were clear, I would nip hastily across to the next covered spot. This tiring process took us around in several small circles as I got lost, and failed to find any of our opponents. Eventually we lost the game because our time limit expired. So we tried again. With each game, we became bolder: we were less cautious before running into the open; we took more risks; and still we took too long, got lost, and lost the game. And still we had not found any of our enemies. Far from being some happy multi-national gaggle of computer players all looking for a game, it seemed as though, in the entire world, only Manfred and I wanted to play "counter-strike," and even when working as a team, we could not beat our non-existent opponents.

It was now past 1.30am. We left that game, and went in search of some cyber friends to play with. It turned out that there were many other people playing; they just hadn't wanted to join our game. I don't really understand how these things work, but we scanned lists of other games that were already going on, looking for the number of players in them, and asking if we could join in. Most of the games that had any decent number of people playing also had a sinister picture of a padlock next to them, telling us that we were not welcome. We tried others and were told that our computer lacks some incomprehensible "dod" drive or something, and so we were not wanted there either. Eventually we managed to get 'in' to a couple of games, but we were only allowed as spectators. Watching this happy little international cyber community blow the shit out of each other with imaginary weapons was a singularly unfulfilling exercise. And after half an hour, we gave up on it.

It seemed that the Internet gaming community is just as impenetrable as any social scene. If you just turn up and ask desperately if *anyone* wants to play with you, then you just get laughed at. "What a loser!" they all think, which is odd, considering that they are a community of people who play computer games all night. But that bitchy thought was no consolation at the time. The fact was that I did want to join their community, no matter how pathetic I might normally think that it was. And they wouldn't let me, the bastards.

It was now past 3am, and we still hadn't got a proper game. So we had a go at something called 'star craft' that I didn't understand at all. Manfred was very good at it, and kept beating me so easily that it was almost as if he was playing on his own. We didn't seem to be able to play this against the Internet community either. I was starting to get very bored. I looked around me. There didn't actually seem to be that many people here. Was the whole idea of the Chinese loving to play computer games all night just a myth?

“Maybe it’s the wrong night; Tuesday night can’t be their busiest night,” mused Manfred. We played on for another couple of hours, keen to complete the ‘all-nighter’ now that we had come this far. But it wasn’t any fun. The computers were slow, and besides, I don’t like computer games. Eventually at 5.30, we tried to leave. I say tried, because it turned out at this stage that leaving was not as simple as you may expect. The front door onto the street was locked. The back door was locked. We woke up the girl curled up behind the desk, who sent us to a fire escape door upstairs. That was also locked. I was tired, disgruntled, and wanted to be in my bed, and not in a grimy, smoky Internet café. Eventually we managed to get a friendly chap to go into a back office to wake up a manager figure who then went downstairs to get a key from someone else, and then finally could open the fire escape door. Their whole attitude was one of “eh? People leaving the café? That’s odd, why would you want to do that?” It turns out that the doors to the place are shut at 10 or 11, and if you are not in by then, then you are not coming in. Similarly, if you are in at that time, then you are expected not to leave. This was the reason that the first cafes that we went to were shut; we had missed their cut off time. And this is also surely a part of the reason why they stay at these places all night; at 10pm they are still keen for another game, and that means that they are in there until dawn.

I can’t say that I learned anything of any importance from my little cultural experimentation. I don’t like staying up all night. I don’t like computer games; I can’t see them as anything other than a total waste of time. Maybe they do use it an escape from their mundane lives. But for escapism purposes, I would rather get blind drunk any time. If there is a happy little cyber-community of games players from all over the world enjoying some harmless fun together, then good luck to them. But I think that they are very boring, and that isn’t just because they spurned me. I don’t think.

Chapter 34

I was once again thumbing through the Qiqihaer tourist guide, when my eye fell upon the description of Tazi town. This, the pamphlet claimed, has a 7.9 metre-high main city wall, going the whole 4.75 km around the town. The wall is from the Liao dynasty – the same period as the piece of "great wall" that I have found on maps that separates Heilongjiang from Inner Mongolia. This could sound like an interesting place for a visit, to anyone unfamiliar with Chinese tourist sites. But for me this place held another form of interest: the pamphlet was produced in 1989, and they were clearly pitching this place as a tourist destination. I wanted to know if they had had any success at all; I looked for Tazi on the map, and it was very remote from any place of any importance. Could they have managed to tempt people out here to have a look at their mud wall? The pamphlet claimed that "a two hour trip by train will bring visitors from Qiqihaer to Tai Lai County seat. Five regular buses are available from Tai Lai to Tazi town." But it didn't tell me that those buses took three hours. I had to find that out for myself.

I very nearly didn't go to Tazi. I woke up feeling that a few more hours in bed were likely to be a great deal more rewarding than trudging alone around an ancient mud wall. But then I remembered how bad I had felt the week before after doing nothing all weekend; if I had to be stuck in Qiqihaer, I thought, I may as well make as much of it as I could. So I went.

The train was packed as usual. I know there are a lot of people in China, but it nonetheless amazes me every time I discover that there are actually a full train load of people trying to get from Qiqihaer to some other non-destination. And this time, there were even those who had booked too late, and were going to have to stand. I found that astonishing.

At Tai Lai, the enormous square in front of the station was filled with, on the left-hand side, fleets of red Volkswagon Santanas, and on the right, hoards of bright yellow three-wheeled bubble cars. It was a strange sight. But Tai Lai seemed to be a surprisingly thriving city. There were clean new apartment blocks going up, and I even saw a coffee shop that didn't look too unpleasant.

"So this," I thought to myself, "is the transfer hub for all those who wish to go to the historical sight of Tazi." But it was clear from the excitement caused by the arrival of a foreigner on the bus that not many of us make the trip up there. The bus conductor checked my ticket four or five times, so disbelieving was he that I should want to go to Tazi. Quite where he thought that I should want to go from Tai Lai isn't clear. As I got onto the bus, a young lad leapt up and thrust his hand into mine, and started talking. These conversations are always fairly similar throughout Dongbei, but the conversations that happen in each specific smaller area are even more similar to each other. This lad gave me my first taste of the 'Tai Lai county foreigner conversation.' It goes more or less like this:

1. "This place is very poor"
2. "What do you do in China?" plus relevant questions about which university, etc.
3. "How much does it cost to go to university?"
4. "Do you Study English there?"
5. "How much did you flight to Qiqihaer cost?"
6. "How much will you earn when you go back to England?"
7. "Do you have any English pounds?

I had a twenty pound note with me, so I often relented and pulled it out, waiting patiently as it is passed around the bus/ restaurant/ shop to whoever wants to see it. This gives rise to the next comment:

8. “You will find it very hard to buy anything in Tazi with English pounds; no one will change them.”

They then found it very hard to believe that I used Chinese money; I am a foreigner, after all, I must use only foreign money.

9. “Have you ever eaten Chinese food?”

We chatted away in this manner for the next hour and a half. He told me about the old town wall at Tazi, which I found quite exciting – a true confirmation of its existence. Then, after a brief pause in conversation, he stood up, picked up his things, and got off the bus. He never said goodbye or turned around once to wave. He just trotted off across the field. Good-byes are almost always like this in China. No sentimentality, no fuss. Just get on with it. It is quite upsetting in a way to begin with, but once you are used to it, it makes the whole process much less awkward; no need to exchange numbers, or pretend that you are going to meet again. Just go on your way.

The bus stopped at a checkpoint, where an official came on to count how many of us there were, and whether the right number of tickets had been sold. My fellow passengers, who had by now adopted me as a sort of a mascot, shrieked in excitement.

“Look! Look! We’ve got a foreigner!” they chimed. I did my best to look modest about my position as bus mascot, but I needn’t have bothered; the official was far too important to be interested by such things as foreigners. He gave me a haughty “well, I hope you’ve bought a ticket” look, and moved grumpily on. The excitement of the other passengers was touching though, and it reminded me of another comment that was often made when I came across people who had not seen a Westerner before: after talking for a while, they would start repeating “my god! A foreigner! Isn’t it amazing?” to me, in hushed tones. Having shared a conversation, they seemed to then expect me to share their amazement in the fact that I was a foreigner. “My word, so I am!” I am supposed to say. “Christ, well that *is* a surprise; who’d of thought it? Me – a foreigner?” The thought that I have had to live for my *entire* life as a foreigner to the Chinese is not one that they seem to be able to entertain.

After lunching in a dingy restaurant, watched by crowds of amazed onlookers conducting the standard conversation, I went in search of the town wall. It still forms the boundary of the town, and it is still quite impressive. It has, unsurprisingly, fallen deep into disrepair; at times, it just looks like a big mound of earth. But in places, you can still see the brickwork, and you can still imagine what it was once like. There is a main inner wall, then a moat, and then a smaller outer wall. The moat has long since dried up, and now sheep graze in it, shepherded by an old man with a pockmarked face.

I stood on the top of the wall, looking on one side out across the brown and dusty plain towards the foothills of Inner Mongolia, and on the other side looking back into the patchwork of paddy fields and mud houses the make up the town. The wind whipped cotton wool clouds across the sun, and their black shadows gave the place a dramatic and almost epic feel; I gazed out to the North, and half expected to see the Mongol hoards descending from the hills. It hadn’t, I suspected, had anything like that level of excitement or importance for hundreds of years, but in other respects, life there had probably changed little in that time. In China, people always talk of the 800 million peasant farmers who make up the bulk of the population, but if you stick to the cities, and sometimes in China it seems almost impossible to escape them, you are obviously unlikely to see too many. Tazi is the quintessential Chinese town in this respect; it is not so much a town in the Western sense, but more a tightly packed collection of tiny farms. Each household seemed to have its own paddy field; many have a couple of pigs, and maybe a mule.

The yellow headscarf of a middle-aged woman digging irrigation ditches in her field caught my eye. The sharp contrast of the brown earth of the countryside and buildings with the rich green of the field and the bright yellow scarf made me reach for my camera. I noticed that she was looking up, and so decided to take the picture as subtly as I could; I didn't want to offend her, but I could scarcely ask her if it was ok from this distance. She held her gaze, and started to walk towards me. I decided to go and have a chat. She was a smiling middle aged woman, who must have been quite pretty in her youth. She didn't ask the usual questions, but instead started to tell me about the wall. "It is over a thousand years old," she said, and asked me if I was interested in history. For most Chinese, an interest in History is an anathema, and I liked the fact that this woman seemed to be an exception. She invited me in to her bungalow – a three-room affair covered in shining white tiles. We sat on the kang and chatted about her daughter, who was studying English.

"But we never have a chance to speak English," she complained.

"What?" I feigned surprise, "are there not many Western tourists around here?"

"You are the first foreigner that I have ever seen," and so she shattered the illusion of the tourist Mecca. Her elderly and toothless aunt then came home, and looked so frail and so utterly non-comprehending that I worried that she may have a heart attack. She looked at me in dumb shock, and for a few minutes was scarcely able to utter a word. The first woman then left to go back to work in the field. I longed to be able to ask the aunt about her life; she can't have been a day under 80, and must have had a fascinating story to tell. But once again my limitations were made abundantly clear. Conversation dwindled, and I excused myself to continue my ramble around the wall.

The tourist guide had spoken of watchtowers at the corners, which was simply a lie. And I couldn't find the ruins of the supposed Zhou dynasty temple that the book claimed was there. But I didn't need to find these things to be impressed by the town. It was quite awesome in a way. And the fact that there were no other tourists, and no effort to make it a tourist sight made it all the more exciting. The people were the friendliest and kindest that I had yet met, and that was high praise in a country where almost everyone had shown me incredible hospitality – with the single notable exception of Mr Guo: the man whose job it was to look after me.

On the bus back to Tai Lai, we stopped to let a young boy of about 16 get on. He left another boy standing by the road, and as they parted they held hands for a lingering moment. This surprised me, as I had never seen such a heart-felt goodbye in China. The boy left on the road was crying, and the boy on the bus sat at the very back, and gazed out of the rear window for as long as his friend was in sight. When he turned around again, his eyes were also full of tears. My curiosity burned; what could the story be? I guessed that he might be going away to the city to school, and wouldn't be back for a long time. But his only luggage was a length of yellow wire, a tin mug in a bag, and what looked like a plastic jubilee clip, still in its cellophane wrapper. Could this really be his luggage? I resolved to ask him when we arrived in Tai Lai, but after another five miles or so, he left us, and wandered his lonely way back to a collection of mud huts at the end of a long poplar avenue.

Later I learned a little more about Tazi from a photograph I took of a sign on one of the town's gates. It was written in traditional Chinese characters and it took Diana and Joseph quite some time to translate it. It turned out that the first mention that there was a city there was in about 1000 AD. At that time, it was called "Feng Zhou." A tribe of the Qi Dan nation called the 'black rats' had taken over the city, and was pillaging everything. Therefore many citizens had fled 600 miles south to find a new place to live. It seems an inauspicious start to the official history of the place. A powerful general then put the place on the map in about 1030 when he decided to use the area to grow crops for his troops. He put up a big tower and pagoda replete with ornate carvings. This must be what the Qiqihaer guide had claimed was a Zhou dynasty tower. It was in fact put up during the local Jin dynasty, which was the dynasty founded by the Qi Dan nation. During the Qing Dynasty, the town was renamed “Tazi” after the Jin Dynasty tower. In 1953, the tower fell down, but apparently the remains are still visible. They must be pretty well hidden is all I can say. So it seems that when I suggested that the times of importance were long gone for Tazi, I was in fact wrong in assuming that there ever had been a time of its importance; it was always a crappy little town. And the very structure that it was named after fell over fifty years ago, after standing for nearly a thousand years. Once I had found all of this out, I wanted to go back and have another look at it. I felt that it had lied to me in its pretence of fallen grandeur, and I wanted to see it as it really was; but I didn’t, and I doubt that I ever will.

Chapter 35

For Sunday lunch one day at the end of May we went for a picnic on Mingyue Dau. A troop of about twenty or so of us – Buriat Russians, Austrians, Chinese, Americans, Koreans and me – trekked from the pier where the ferry docked, for about three-quarters of an hour through some really quite beautiful countryside. I say trekked; there was of course a pristine new concrete road, but it was hot, and it seemed like a long way. It was a flat island, speckled with crystal lakes and groves of poplars, birches and various other trees that I cannot name.

Traditional style temples built in the 1920s rose up above the trees every hundred yards or so. There were some 'tourist attractions' such as the being-led-in-a-small-circle-whilst-sitting-on-a-camel-or-a-horse gag that I had fallen foul of before. But it was a huge island, and these little glitches were swallowed up in the immensity of what was, for the most part, an unspoiled wilderness. And there were no plastic bags! Imagine my excitement. There were bins placed every few hundred yards, and they seem to be being used. This was clearly a surprise not only to me, but also to whoever it was that designed the bins; they were moulded out of concrete ('tastefully' into the shape of a tree trunk) and had a tiny opening in the top for you to pop your rubbish into. But I took the time to examine one more closely, and found that there was no way to get the rubbish out again once the time comes to empty it. They clearly thought that this would never be a problem that they were likely to encounter. The concept of disposable bins seemed quaintly ridiculous.

We picked up a tourist guide from the ferry that was once again written in the most wonderful English. It suggested some hilarious ‘tour items’ on the island, beginning by listing a whole load of pavilions, and then going on “…The General Mansion The Exhibition of crane city appearance diagram slice the production base of green food.” Try re-punctuating it any way you like; that does not make sense. Under the ‘amusement items,’ we were tantalised by suggestions that we may visit the “International standard tennis place, Glasses lake-Fishing place, Racecourse, The double-men and triple-men’s bicycle, Yurt, Washing your hands in gold basin, The landscape trendy photography wedding cloths…” and so on. Sadly, we were unable to find the “wash your hands in gold basin,” or, indeed, any of these truly wonderful sounding attractions.

We did, however, find a shaded spot next to a small lake, far away from any other. We set up a barbecue, and the Buriat girls knocked up a delicious salad. We had an array of spices for the meat, and a loaf of Russian bread with which you could make something not totally unlike a sandwich. Dawei had brought some vodka, and periodically forced people to drink some with him. Only he really had too much though, and soon he was down to his tiny Y-fronts and in the lake, thrashing merrily around. As we sat watching him, sipping iced tea in the cool of the shade, a realisation that had been forming for some time crystallised in my mind: Qiqihaer really was a very nice place to live, at least in the summer.

As well as that, I felt then that I could almost understand why all those Chinese people want to move from their beautiful little town like Tazi to the ‘big city:’ it is prosperous, and it is, compared to Tazi, glamorous. They can still ‘enjoy the countryside’ when they want. They can go to discos if the want. And they probably *can* enjoy a better “standard of living” (whatever that means). Just as I was considering this, and how different a sort of ‘enjoying the countryside’ this was to the farming that I saw in Tazi yesterday, Dawei’s girlfriend (sadly we all kept forgetting her name, and so she remained ‘Dawei’s girlfriend’ for as long as I knew her) complained that this was a boring, empty place. She was a very sweet girl, and I liked her, but she ruined my little dream of empathizing with the Chinese. They clearly didn't view Mingyue Dau as a haven. They viewed it as a boring, empty place. Maybe that is why there is no rubbish; no one had been there. Among the Chinese that we had with us, only two had ever been there before, and then only when they were five or six years old. There were a lot of people on the ferry to go over to the island, but since we hadn't seen any actually on the island; I can only assume that they had all found a little corner of the island to bustle about in. So whatever their reasons are for wanting to move to Qiqihaer, they are not the same as the reasons that made it such an agreeable place for me.

Chapter 36

Having spent my first three months running for cover whenever I spied anyone who looked like they might be looking for a 'language partner,' I now picked up two in quick succession. The first was a friend of Manfred's. I was looking for a tutor to help me with my spoken Chinese, and Manfred suggested Lishanshan. She had helped him when he was starting to learn Chinese, and he recommended her as being a good teacher. But at our first lesson, just as I was trying to make the best possible effort to ingratiate myself, she slipped in the suggestion that instead of paying her we should do alternate lessons; one time she would teach me Chinese, one time I would teach her English. I really only wanted a tutor, but a moment of weakness was all it took, and I had agreed.

That was the first language partner; the second one was Nannan. I was having a quiet lunch on my own at my favourite restaurant, when the owner rushed up to me and started babbling as I was happily engaged with a plate of noodles. In my eagerness to eat, I didn't really listen to what she was rabbiting on about, and decided to go for the 'nod and look pleased' way out of having to say anything. Soon she got up and left me alone, and I was just congratulating myself on a peace well won, when she returned with a burly Chinese girl intent on chatting. I put down my chopsticks and resigned myself to actually having to make conversation. After a couple of minutes, I discovered that I had expressed a keenness to indulge in a language exchange with her. The main problem with these exchanges is that they refuse to ever talk in Chinese, so rather than an exchange, it becomes a simple English lesson. I decided to test the water.

"How good is your English?" I annunciated as carefully as I could.

"Shenme?" she asked, which means "what," and this was accompanied by a startled and confused look.

"How good…" the look was still there, so I gave up and switched into Chinese.

"Oh!" she laughed, finally understanding, "NO!"

This seemed like good news to me. She clearly couldn't speak a single word. (Other than "No," which, you will have noticed, she used incorrectly anyway.) So I gladly agreed to a lesson the next day, and slipped back to the dormitory.

Although I fell into both of these arrangements without meaning to, it was partly the result of an intentioned plan. I had decided that as my spoken Chinese was beginning to reach a passable level, I would gain more out of a language exchange than I would have done before. They would, I hoped, help me to learn how to interact in everyday situations more effectively than the unrealistic scenarios given in the textbook.

My first lesson with Lishanshan took place in the night market. The market is a bustling crowd that took over the main road into town from about 5 o'clock every day once the warm weather had arrived. Endless stalls sold enormous pairs of Y-fronts and abbidas (sic) tracksuit bottoms. The smells of the street mingled with the smells of a thousand different types of exotic street food, and at times, it was for a moment hard to decide whether a new pungent aroma was that of a delicious barbecue, or a rotting carcass. Lishanshan was tiny and bouncy. Normally she went a few paces in front of me, and bobbed along in a jolly little backwards skip as she taught. In the crowd of the market, she took to weaving in and out of the legs of the taller Chinese as I struggled even to keep up, let alone to hear what it was that she was explaining. Lacking her manoeuvrability, I bumbled along in a flurry of apologies and "excuse me"s, my ears straining to pick out her pearls of wisdom above the din. Every few hundred yards, she would stop to make some notes for me in my notebook, and I would try to hold her in conversation for a minute about whichever bric-a-brac stall we happened to have paused by. It gradually transpired that there wasn't really anything worth buying but as I got the hang of cutting through the crowd, and began to keep up, we were able to look at things of some interest, which she could explain, and sometimes I could hear. I liked having a lesson like that. And afterwards, I had twenty or so phrases stuffed with new words, which I learned and then wheeled out on every future visit to a market.

When I could hear her, Lishanshan was a good teacher; she could speak English, but she always preferred to make me speak Chinese. And she had a gift for explaining things. She was good company, and she was a communist party member which I found fascinating. Members have to be at the top of their class, and then have to get about 70% of their classmates to vote for them in order to get in to the Party. Quite democratic really, in a way. I don't think that she was a particularly fervent communist, and she was always prepared to discuss anything. But being a party member is a very useful way to get ahead in China.

At one stall selling tacky wooden jewellery, I discovered another example of the similar-sounding-words-making-things-lucky phenomenon. This time it was a small axe with some messy characters carved on it. The characters read "yi fu ya bai huo." The "fu" is from "fu tou" – an axe, but it sounds like the "fu" from "xing fu," which means happy. So the axe is, from what I could make out, a lucky instrument. The whole sentence means, "one axe can prevent a hundred accidents." I am no fan of the 'nanny state' approach of printing warnings on everything that might possibly cause harm – like the coffee cups from fast food shops that now have to have "caution – hot" stamped on them. But it seems to me that printing "one axe can prevent a thousand accidents" on an axe is really going a little too far towards the opposite extreme, even if it is only a toy axe.

The change in my preferred learning style was also evident in the attitude that I began to take to everyday conversations. To begin with, I used to eat my dinner praying that I would be left in peace. I avoided eye contact and tried to remain aloof. I justified this saying that I didn't like small talk and I only liked to practice my language skills when I was fully prepared. Now that I had nearly passed that stage, I could almost admit to myself that it had probably been a simple case of my not liking the feeling of helplessness and stupidity that goes with most language-learning conversations, rather than anything more justifiable. Now that I felt confident at the basics, it was exciting to try to express myself more fully. The learning process was – at long last – becoming something of a pleasure.

Chapter 37

My trip in search of the Oroqen with Ardis was dealt an early blow when we went to buy our tickets at the train station, only to discover that there were no sleeper tickets available. So we had to buy hard-seater tickets for the full seventeen hours. Much as I have learned to enjoy the gritty hurly-burly of the hard sleeper, that carriage does at least afford you the minimal comfort and even 'privacy' of a shelf on which to lie. In the hard-seater you are wedged in between two (you will inevitable get the middle seat), quite probably smelly, coughing, farting and spitting Chinese for the duration. One or other of them is sure to fall asleep and dribble on you. That is just a little bit more of an experience than I really wanted. Or at least it was to begin with; after a while I started to get used to the idea. There is a certain attraction in taking a long journey in the worst class available on what is quite probably the most underdeveloped train line in the country. Surely it would be worth having a look at? And it wasn't like it was actually dangerous.

Or so I thought. Just as I had become comfortable, and even a little excited by the idea, I got a call from Ardis telling me that it was all off. Her mother had decreed that the hard-seater was far too dangerous and that we had to go sleeper. I was a little irritated by this interference; in spite of the ever-accumulating evidence to the contrary (Shaun was mugged and quite badly beaten up the week before), I did still view it as a very safe place. And I didn't like the fact that this interfering mother was going to scupper my plans for a gritty journey. Quite apart from that, we had already tried to buy a hard-sleeper ticket, and there weren't any. Was the whole expedition to be called off? No. The great Chinese system of "guanxi" (connections) came into play. Ardis' mother knew the head of the train station. We waited next to a closed window in the ticket office (there was rather a quaint little sign reading “back in a jiffy,” as a translation for the stern Chinese characters reading simply “Wait here), and within minutes the blind was lifted up, and we had two of the supposedly non-existent hard-sleeper tickets being thrust into our hands. I like it when the system works for you.

As I drove back through the streets of Qiqihaer, I gazed at the signs above the restaurants. I have longed for the day that these confusions of lines would inflate with meaning and all would become clear. “There is a chemist! There is an insurance company!” I would say with authority. And then all of a sudden, I started to notice that I did understand quite a lot. I wouldn’t go so far as to say that the characters leapt off the signs and danced with meaning; but if I stared at a character for a few moments, what started as a feeling of dim recognition, as with the face of a childhood friend who has not been seen for many years, slowly grew into actual recognition, a sound would pop into my head, and the meaning would appear. There were very few signs that I could read in their entirety, but I could work out what many of them were getting at. The trip down the dull high street became an adventure of discovery. Suddenly I could make decent guesses as to what the shops might sell. Scarcely an earth-shattering achievement, but an encouraging one.

As I sat in the photo shop, proudly showing off the new vocabulary that Li Shan Shan had taught me for the occasion, I noticed an elderly Chinese man who looked exactly like the racehorse trainer Sir Michael Stout. Perhaps it was the familiarity of his face, but I decided that I liked him, and tried to engage him in conversation. When he spoke his voice was a sort of gurgling bubbling sound that came from deep in his throat. It was not unlike the sound of a baby being tickled, but much deeper. Quite incomprehensible of course, but rather cheering. Eventually I worked out that the problem of his extraordinary voice was compounded by a terrible stutter; not an affliction that I had come across before in China, but then I suppose that I hadn’t spoken to enough people. Once I had cracked the code, talking with him once again became a pleasure. Sadly his bus arrived and he left me before I had a chance to broach the subject of his famous English twin brother, and so unless Sir Michael can shed any light on his gurgling twin in Dongbei, then it will have to remain forever a mystery.

While asleep at my studies the next morning, I was roused from my slumbers by the sound of Ardis calling my telephone.

"Where are you?" she sounded flustered. Had I arranged to meet her?

"The train leaves in twenty minutes!" Had I slept right through Wednesday and into Thursday morning? No. It transpired that I had told Ardis the wrong date. I had said that we should buy the tickets for Thursday, and had taken a wild guess at the date. She had taken the date as the correct figure (an excusable mistake, I suppose; she simply couldn't understand that I had to think for a moment to work out what month it was, let alone what the *exact* date was), and had booked them for Wednesday. I frantically struggled to work out whether I could just throw some things in a bag and head off, but as I prevaricated, the cut off time to get on the train was approaching, and the station was still a fifteen minute taxi ride away. I had clearly missed the train. There was nothing for it but to accept full responsibility, pay for both of our replacement tickets, and try to beg forgiveness.

When I arrived at the station, Ardis had once again been in contact with her friend in high places, who had agreed to exchange our tickets without charge, which seemed unnecessarily good of him. So we went to have lunch while we waited for him. Ardis had an improbable amount of luggage for this short sortie. She was loaded down with presents for her relations, including 700 kuai's (about £50) worth of baijiu. This seemed an enormous amount to have spent on something so categorically disgusting, and since a bottle of baijiu is generally available for about fifty pence, it also seemed to suggest a truly stupefying quantity. In fact she had originally bought just four bottles (which had cost 1400 in total) of 'top quality' but she dropped one of them and smashed it. Since it is bad luck to give three of anything to someone as a present, she had had to leave one bottle at home for a rainy day, and give them two bottles instead. People prefer to be given the more auspicious number of two bottles than the larger number of three bottles, which doesn't seem sensible to me, foolish capitalist and materialist that I am. I asked to take a look at these costly bottles of vomit-inducement, and I must admit that that they had done a fair job of dressing it up; it looked pretty exotic. As I examined it, Ardis again worried me by suggesting that I would be expected to get stuck in to one or both of the bottles with her relatives.

"Dongbei people have a saying: "yi jiu hui you," " she told me. Roughly translated it means, "closer friends drink more together," or something similar. Her basic message was that if you don't drink a simply mind-bending amount, then you are not real friends, and that her family would expect to be treated like real friends. It is strange: when I was in Shanghai there was a generally believed myth that the Chinese lack certain alcohol-digesting enzymes, and so are unable to drink very much. It is true that in Shanghai, the Chinese don't seem to drink very much alcohol. But although Dongbeiren are particularly keen on getting the right side of a bottle or two, I think that the phenomenon is more widespread than just this area. Mo Yan, one of China's best contemporary authors, wrote a novel called 'Republic of Wine' about his homeland. The book was founded on the obsession with alcohol that abounds here (it also has quite a lot of stuff about eating babies that I sincerely hope is less based in reality.) Whatever the truth about which parts of China are obsessed with alcohol, the fact remains that I was deep in the heart of the stronghold of alcoholism, and the trip north promised to be a liver-punishing affair.

Ardis and I finally caught the train North on Thursday morning. I had a splitting headache and was desperately tired; a farewell barbecue for Manfred had ended rather late. It was a bad way to start a 17-hour rain journey with a companion I hardly knew. I contented myself with re-reading the material that George had given me on the History and Language of the Oroqen. I couldn't really focus – a job made more difficult by the jolting of the train – but it kept me away from the need for conversation. After an hour though, I gave up and climbed up to the middle bunk to try to have a snooze. In the bunk above me a tiny mother and child played noisily. I envied them the ability to manoeuvre in such a tiny space; it took me about thirty seconds of wriggling just to roll over. In other compartments, people raised their voices to chat over the clunking of the train, and outside the grasslands rolled quietly past. Surrounded by the hubbub and yet just an observer from my bunk, I felt very content, and soon fell asleep.

I was awoken about two hours later by a beaming Chinese man clutching my foot. I couldn't work out if he had made an honest mistake in reaching for the bedpost for support, or if this was a hideously misled effort at ingratiating himself. If it was the latter, it failed. I shot him the sternest glare that I could manage through my confusion, and then turned to stare stubbornly out of the window. The grasslands had given way to enormous brown fields marked out by stately avenues of poplars and muddy tracks. We were only a couple of hours out of Qiqihaer, and the lilacs were back in bloom. We seemed to have travelled back in time by about two weeks. I harboured high hopes that by the end of the journey we would have moved right back to winter; Ardis' uncle had told her that in Ta Er Gen (his village) there was still snow on the ground, and the trees were still bare. This may have been true at the time that we boarded the train, but sadly the seasons caught up with us; when I woke again at 4 am, it had been sunrise for an hour already and green hills were poking through the mist. It was a spring morning. When we passed villages, people were already up tilling their tiny fields, and for the first time I saw that some of them were still wearing Mao suits. "This is what communist China must have looked like," I thought, but then I saw a young woman in high heels and a shapely trouser-suit herding goats. It seemed a strange mix of styles.

When we finally arrived in Ta Er Gen, where Ardis's uncle and aunt lived, I went almost straight to bed; it was, after all, 4.30 am. I roused myself at 8.30 to find Ardis ready and prepared to go for a walk in the forest. This seemed like rather a good plan to me. I was also thrilled that of all the Chinese people that I could have come to the mountains with, I seemed to have picked one who was not totally confused by the idea of walking anywhere. I had started to notice before that Ardis was not like most Chinese people. The first sign of this was her fear of chickens. We were walking to a restaurant one day, when she suddenly froze, almost stiff, but just trembling slightly. I had walked on a few paces before I noticed, but I didn't immediately want to draw attention to the situation, so I awkwardly waited for a few moments hoping that it would right itself. It became clear that there would be no such easy way out, and I sauntered carefully closer, not sure whether she was going to drop dead or bite me. Just as I was reaching out a tentative finger to give her a prod, she came back to life and scuttled away in the opposite direction, muttering about chickens. I looked behind me and saw that as I had walked closer, I had blocked her from the chickens that were wandering around the lane, and so had released her from her 'rabbit in headlights' freeze. I had to herd the clucking beasts out of the way before she could dart in for lunch.

This fear of the Chinese staple food had already started me thinking and then on the train, she just seemed to be a little bit *prissy*. She didn't enter into the pyjama wearing, chatting, spitting and eating fun that was second nature for the others. She seemed to want some privacy, and tried to avoid talking to the other people. She constantly washed her hands with dainty little wipes, and while she didn't recoil in quite the way that I often do when a passer by threw out a huge globule of phlegm onto the floor of our compartment, she did seem a little put out. I started to think about the other young Chinese that I know. Actually, I can't think of a single one of them that would hoick and spit in the way that their parents do. Maybe it is just another relic of the Cultural Revolution: a time when children told their parents what to do, and that with the rise of the younger generation, it will disappear.

The uncle had pulled some strings to get us through the fire checkpoints (spring is the main time for forest fires, and normally no one is allowed into the forest at all with out very good reason) and we set off through the woods next to the Ta river. It was a gurgling torrent, about seventy metres wide, and I was sure that it was packed with fish. I cursed myself for having left my rod behind, and decided to ask the uncle about fishing when we got back. In places the rolling hills to our left actually became quite dramatic, with jutting rock formations and crumbling cliffs that were far beyond anything that hills of their meagre height should have held. The birds were singing, there was no one around for miles, and I was starting to enjoy myself when, after about fifteen minutes, Ardis called a halt.

“Shall I call them?” she asked.

“Who?”

“My uncle. I call them and they will come and pick us up in the taxi. They say that there is a beautiful view here, but I can’t find it.” I thought that it was all beautiful enough, but I wasn’t going to force her to go on; I was by now used to these little disappointments. Besides, I was sure that if this was all that had been planned for our ‘walk in the woods’ then they must have had other entertainments in mind.

When the uncle arrived, I asked him about the fishing. He was a portly clay-model of a man whose head seemed to have been thrust on by an over-enthusiastic child. When he was excited, he wobbled as his arms flailed.

“Loads of fish!” he cried with glee. “We catch them by…” and the rest was incomprehensible to me. Although he did point repeatedly at what I had previously taken to be a fording point in the river. I asked Ardis for a translation. She looked a little sheepish.

"They throw in a bomb, and catch the fish as they go through that place." She pointed at a gap in the ford where the main current was channelled.

Over lunch I was reminded of how little I understood. There were mitigating factors acting against me; for example, the local accent is not totally standard. But the main problem was that it was a group of Chinese people talking the Chinese that they talk to each other, and not the simplified stuff that they talk to foreigners. And so it all rushed over my head. Often I could understand enough words to work out what they were talking about, but I would just miss enough to be unable to work out what they were actually saying about the subject. So I sat in a contented silence for most of the meal, only stirring to accept a "ganbei!" We had been waiting a while for the special dish of the day – some locally bombed fish – to be produced, when Ardis turned to me and said in English, "I hope that the fish is worth waiting for."

"They have probably gone out to catch it," I quipped lamely. She found this hilarious, and in a well-intentioned effort to show to the others that I was more than just a moronic silent giant, she translated it to them. A table full of silent and offended faces turned slowly from Ardis's giggling face to my blushing one. "Are you insulting our hospitality? Is our restaurant not good enough for you? You westerners are so damned impatient!" they seemed to be thinking. After a good few moments registering their disapproval, conversation slowly seeped back to the table. When no one would notice Ardis turned to me.

"Sorry," she whispered, and looked desperate. I just smiled though; I had been mortified when I had first realised that she was translating my comments to them, but by now I was just finding the situation amusing. At times it did seem that Ardis was just as at sea in this company as I was.

When we got back to Ta Er Gen after lunch we went to see a deer farm. I was excited to see that there were at least some of them left, but I wanted to know if there would be enough left in the wild to support the hunting of the Oroqen if they ever wished to return to their nomadic lifestyle.

"Are there many deer left in the wild?" I asked, but the keeper didn't seem to understand. I tried a couple more times, and eventually persuaded Ardis to ask. The idea horrified her. "These enormous animals! Allowed to run free? Horrible!" seemed to be her attitude. And sure enough when the keeper was asked, he just laughed at the absurdity of the notion. But not only is there nothing left for the Oroqen to shoot; it is also illegal to own a gun.

Chapter 38

The first Oroqen woman that I met was sitting on a plastic-covered sofa watching television in her government-built house in Shibazhan. She had tightly permed black hair like Dot from Eastenders. “We hate living in the village” she said, “we are a hunting people.” She spoke Oroqen, and she told us that the children were taught to speak it in the schools. But her granddaughter couldn’t speak a word, or even understand it. She told us that in spite of the law, she still owned a gun. And some of the men still went out hunting; there were twenty hunters left between this village and Baiyina, the other nearby settlement.

The houses that have been built for them by the government contravene many of the Oroqen traditions. Some of the older Oroqen still believe that they will contract strange diseases if they sleep inside, and make their own shelters outside the house. The younger ones, however seem to have lost these traditional ways and along with them, it seems, their will to live: a couple of years ago, there was a fire in the village and everyone was evacuated from their houses. “Take all your valuables!” they were told. They all trekked out into the night carrying their enormous flasks of baijiu. That was the only thing that they really cared about.

We walked around the village for a while, looking in at occasional houses, and ‘admiring’ their handicrafts; every ethnic minority needs a little handicraft to sell, and for the Oroqen it was little plates, pots and tea pots made out of the bark of birch trees, decorated with a weaving braid pattern that is apparently sacred to the Oroqen. They were not entirely unpleasant, but obviously quite naff. The Uncle asked me if I liked anything, and I pointed to a tea set and tried to appear enthusiastic. Before I knew what was happening, he had handed over 300 kuai and bought the wretched thing for me. It was too embarrassing for words; it was really very expensive. I felt awful, but tried to look thrilled.

By the time we reached Baiyina, the second Oroqen village, our ranks had grown to about ten, including a military escort, and a small museum of Oroqen culture was opened for our benefit. This contained the last examples of their headwear and clothing that are left in the area; a mystery foreigner turned up in the autumn, and bought all the rest, including all of the hunting hats made from deer heads, still replete with antlers. There was a photograph of a woman in full shaman's dress that we were told was the last surviving Oroqen shaman. We wanted to meet her, but were told that she had now moved to Shibazhan, so we had missed her in the morning; we would have to go back and have a look later on, if we had time. The woman that was showing us around the museum turned out to be a keen singer of Oroqen folk songs, and later, at her house, I recorded some videos of her singing to give to George. He had had a romantic notion of recording some of their music before it disappears forever, but had never quite had the time to find them. One of the songs was about a man who went to see his daughter's father in law, and was very angry with him for reasons that I couldn't find out. The other was 'just a love song,' she said. The music was beautiful in its own way, but the sight of that stout woman with thickly painted eyebrows belting it out in front of "wheel of fortune," or whatever rubbish was going on on the television behind her, was hardly the romantic experience I had dreamed of.

The Oroqen youth skulked around the village in tracksuits and smoked. They were indistinguishable from Chinese youth anywhere. Very, very few of them could speak their language, even if they were taught it at school. The old woman with the perm might have talked of 'wanting to be hunters,' but she herself had lived in the village since she was 2 years old, and so could scarcely call herself a nomad. And these children were never going to be hunters.

Nothing could interest them less. The Oroqen culture existed only in the minds of the old people and in the imagination of visitors like myself.

Chapter 39

The mention of the Shaman had fired my imagination; this wise old woman might just have been the life behind the community. While outwardly all appeared depressingly Chinese, behind closed doors they all deferred to this ancient pillar of learning. I imagined her to be like the Storyteller in Mario Vargas Llosa's novel of the same name: an enigmatic figure that shifts around in the dark, telling tales of how life used to be, and keeping alive the dreams of returning to the wild.

This notion was blown out of the water over dinner back in Shibazhan when Ardis' attempts to track the old woman down were thwarted by the news, from several different sources, that she had died. About two years ago. And her devoted followers in Baiyina had not even noticed.

Eventually though, it turned out that she hadn't died; she just didn't like to get out very much. The dream of the pillar of the community was dead, but we went in search of her nonetheless. We found her in a tiny back room (traditionally Oroqen women were not allowed in the back of a dwelling) of a scruffy little bungalow. She was feeling ill, and was not too keen on accepting visitors. She was absolutely tiny. She understood Chinese, but mostly spoke in Oroqen. She did not want to talk about her role as a Shaman.

"We lived for hunting and fishing. Now there is nothing for us," she kept saying. She had made a little paper cut-out of the Oroqen braid pattern, and gave it to me to look at. The pattern had been cut from the dosage instructions to her heart medication pills; the English writing was readable in between the cuts. There seemed to be a powerful image in that, but I still struggle to work out what it is.

Ardis was forced to put on what they claimed was 'traditional Oroqen national dress,' decorated generously with plastic beads that I am sure were not available in the wild. She was mortified. "I am not Oroqen," she kept repeating, and she looked hideously uncomfortable. I liked her for this reluctance to join in with what most Chinese would consider to be the most enjoyable part of the trip. As we left the Shaman, I pointed out my suspicions over the authenticity of the costume. She found the observation very funny, and cheered up. I was just congratulating myself on a job well done when she beetled off and translated it to our guide. Thank god, he didn't take too much offence, but told us that the clothes had been made for the 50th anniversary 'celebration' of their settlement in the village, last year.

"Do you think that they wanted to celebrate, or if they were told to celebrate?" Ardis asked quietly, though she didn't expect me to answer; it was too obvious to say.

Chapter 40

One of the strangest parts of the day was the factory where we ate lunch. This was situated just outside the village of Baiyina, which itself lay 40 kilometres along a terrible dirt road from the end of perhaps the remotest rail line in China. It is about 22 hours by road and rail from Qiqihaer – the nearest city that has even the slightest importance, and which is itself a pretty desolate spot. Quite why this should be a good place to manufacture anything was unclear. The chairman of the factory was a good friend of the uncle, but they had not seen each other for long time, and this was clearly the part of the day that he had most been looking forward to. As we wandered around the smoky, clanking factory, I tried to work out just what it could be making. There were big bags stacked up in the corner containing lumps of something. I just couldn't tell what it was. Ardis kept saying "S.I," but I couldn't work out if that was the name of a product, a company, or what. There seemed to be a big mould that some molten substance was poured into, and allowed to set. This was then removed from the mould, as a big block of silvery metal, and broken into smaller hunks. The job of breaking this down was performed by an elderly man and woman who sat on the floor of a little pen, hammering away at the big chunks. It seemed a very primitive process, whatever it was producing.

When I had a chance, I went back to the car and got my dictionary. I gave it to Ardis. The factory, it turned out, was producing silicon. I have never thought a great deal about the process of producing silicon, but I had certainly never suspected that it might be done like that.

Because they were all such good friends, we had to get very drunk at lunch. The baijiu was out in force, and I left the table with that tingling warmth that only baijiu seems to give you. I don't know how it had happened, but it seemed that suddenly I had learned how to enjoy that filthiest of drinks.

Our final destination for the afternoon was to go and look at Russia over the border, marked by the Heilongjiang river. I have always been rather excited by the Heilongjiang; not only does the name mean 'black dragon river,' but it weaves its remote and mysterious course between Mongolia, Manchuria and Siberia – all places that I can still get childishly excited about just by reading their names.

The river was no disappointment. Even this far from the coast, it was an enormous torrent almost a kilometre wide. And it is fast flowing. In the middle of the river was an island. It was over this island that a brief war was fought in 1969 between the Russians and the Chinese. They had caught two Russian spies just the day before I arrived (quite what they were spying on was never made clear), thus it was somewhat to my surprise that I found myself being allowed into the Chinese army base. This may just have been luck, or it may have been to do with the uncle's connections. But it may also have been to do with the good regard in which the English are held here, due to the actions of one Mr Maxwell. He was an English reporter who came out to cover the war here in 1969, and was apparently very helpful. I have tried without success to find out more about him. Anyway, they seemed pretty pleased with him, and had erected a pagoda in his honour.

At the base, we stood on top of a hill overlooking the river, and a soldier told us about the war.

"The Russians shouted bad things at us from the other side, so we attacked!" he shouted.

"What did they shout?" asked Ardis.

"The island is ours!" said the soldier. That must be the best justification for a war that I have ever heard.

Drunk and tired, but thoroughly pleased with the day's efforts, we headed for home at about 10pm. As we rattled out of Shibazhan, we were stopped at a fire checkpoint, and a torch was thrust through the window to inspect us. I thought smugly of how normal these fire check point procedures now were to me, when two weeks ago I had never known of their existence. But as always, it turned out that I was wrong. This was no fire checkpoint; this was a roadblock set up to find a murderer who had shot someone on the road that evening. I was glad that I hadn't made this trip on my own.

I woke the next morning to find bright sunshine streaming through the window. I went for a walk around the village, and chatted to some locals. They all knew about me, and were all pleased to talk for a while. Some of them spent their days ploughing fields by hand or with horses, while others herded their sheep and goats. They all seemed charmingly happy; but then it was probably the first really warm day of the year, after a bitter winter.

The hills were unassumingly pretty in a hill-next-door sort of way. The forest sometimes looked a little bit *functional*, but that may only be because I knew that they were just a forestry resource. They didn't have the wild and eerie look of a real forest. I did still like it, though. There was an almost Spanish sense of relaxation to these forestry villages and towns that I didn't ever feel elsewhere in China. However, it didn't actually remind me of anywhere that I have been in the world other than Inner Mongolia, and that lies just over the hill. I love both places, and I would have liked to spend more time here. But I had taken too much advantage of their incredible hospitality already, and I had given them very little interesting conversation by way of payment. So we left by the morning train. They even refused to let either myself or Ardis pay for our train tickets, such was their generosity.

As we chatted on the train back, there was none of the awkwardness that there had been at the start of the weekend. She was a quiet girl, but I liked her very much. She did seem to be genuinely interested in the Oroqen culture, and not in the normal Chinese photograph-taking way. And I am certain that my pathetic efforts at improving her spoken English were in no way deserving of the kindness that she showed me in return.

Chapter 41

Guo laoshi marched into my lesson on the Tuesday afternoon of my fourteenth week in Qiqihaer and asked me to interview some prospective teachers to check their English level. I thought that it might be quite amusing, and asked how long it would take. He said that it would 'just' be for three hours on Wednesday and Thursday afternoons. Quite what he thought that I did with my time that I would have two such large gaps at such short notice, I'm not sure. Either way, since I planned to leave for the seaside town of Dalian on Thursday afternoon, I thought that I was off the hook. Mr Gou persisted though, asking again and again, promising cash reward, and cutting the time down to just two hours on Wednesday. Eventually, largely out of a wish to continue the class without interruption, I agreed to help him for two hours on Wednesday for 200 kuai. I wasn't really interested in the money; it was a nice bonus, but I would rather have had my afternoon to myself. It didn't sound too taxing, however; we were just going to watch them teach a prepared lesson, and judge their English. George and Jeremy (an Australian who had lived in Qiqihaer for two years with his local girlfriend, but whom I had only glimpsed once) had been dragged in as well.

On Wednesday I arrived to discover that we were expected to have lists of questions to ask, and that we would be interviewing over thirty candidates. So it wasn't going to be a relaxing afternoon of listening to people speaking English badly, and it certainly wasn't going to be only two hours. I was annoyed with Mr Guo, although not surprised, and wanted to make a fuss. But George and Jeremy were taking the news so stoically that I felt rather shamed and bit my tongue. Liu (George's assistant, and high up in the foreign languages department) seemed to sense that I was in no mood for the job.

"You must not be light hearted," he warned, "for today you have not only the future of these teachers in your hands, but also the futures of all the students that they will teach. Thousands of people depend on your decision." That shut me up, but made me feel worse. How could I be remotely qualified to make this judgement? In one of the weakest attempts to mollify someone that I have ever been subjected to, we were all given brand new Parker pens with which to mark down our comments on each candidate.

The first candidate had a tough time because we really had no idea what to ask. We just sat in an awkward silence while she told us a sob story about her terminally ill grandfather in Qiqihaer, which was the reason that she wanted the job here. If she thought that this would appeal to our kind natures, she was sadly mistaken; we were irritated at being there, and didn't want to listen to her tedious – and probably false – tale of woe. Her English was ungrammatical and jagged and it hurt to listen to her. So we gave her low marks. As the afternoon wore on, we evolved as an interviewing panel. George, being the senior member, gave the introductions, I would then probe them on their hometowns, before Jeremy asked some well thought out brainteasers about teaching techniques. There was a general inflation of marks as we progressed, and we found it harder to pick between people. We had little time to discuss between candidates, and our marks were very rushed. Liu's words rang in our ears, and we didn't want to rush it, but we had no option.

I did start to enjoy hearing about their hometowns, though. This was mainly because of the satisfaction that I derived from being able to nod knowingly when they said that they were from 'Jixi' or somewhere, and say "Ah! Very famous for coal mining, isn't it?" It never impressed the people themselves; of course, *everyone* should know that Jixi is famous for coal mining. But I could see out of the corner of my eye that George and Jeremy were shocked at my seemingly encyclopaedic knowledge of Heilongjiang's minor towns.

"You *are* a spy," George said, after I had just displayed a dazzling knowledge of the taxi system in Tai Lai. I learned more about other towns as well – nuggets of information that I will stow away in the recesses of my mind in the hope that they will some day come in handy. There were several towns that were famous for potatoes, or so we were told. One of the answers we were given by a girl from one of these towns was rather touching in a bizarre sort of a way.

"In my home town, we have potatoes. Many, many potatoes. But few factories; much room to develop." It was a heartfelt opinion, and she nodded sternly as she spoke. I asked a girl from Qiqihaer who had been to University in Harbin what the differences between the cities were.

"Harbin is more developed, more modern."

"In what ways?"

"People buy more clothes." That is one way to judge, I suppose.

We were all three embarrassed by a girl who told us the 'story of the golden apple' as a story that is central to European culture, which she liked to tell to students to arouse their interest. We just couldn't quite place it. She was struggling slightly on the names of Greek gods, which didn't help, but we didn't feel that we could penalise her for that. When she had left we discussed for a few minutes before finally working out that she had been talking about the judgement of Paris. Her superior knowledge of Greek mythology impressed me, and wondered how I ever dared assume that the Chinese don't have an interest in history. In all likelihood, I have only come across such a limited cross section of the population that a similar group in any country would also be fairly uninterested in history.

When the afternoon was over, after five hours of interviewing, they didn't pay us, which didn't surprise me very much. Instead, they invited us to a banquet where I had the 'unrivalled privilege' of sitting next to the Vice President of the University. It was a lively affair, with delicious food, and as much baijiu and karaoke as you would expect. It was also a good opportunity to practice my Chinese, as the Vice President spoke no English at all. But I resented Guo for lying to me once again. And I resented them for stealing my afternoon. That feeling of having had my afternoon stolen from me made me realise just how much I now had to do in Qiqihaer. I couldn't quite pinpoint when or how it had happened, but I did seem to actually have a life there; I had people to meet, places to go and things to do. I was genuinely busy, for the first time in a long time.

Chapter 42

Talking on my telephone is not something that I would ever suggest was a particular hobby of mine back home in England. But in Qiqihaer it became a genuine thrill. I relished the opportunity to call up one of my Chinese friends, and arrange something without speaking English at all. It was immensely satisfying, but also really rather *exciting*. You may say that I led a quiet life there, being excited by things like telephone conversations, and you would probably be right. You may also point out that my conversations are little more than suggesting times and places to meet, and you would also be right. But when I used to watch the Austrians talking on their mobile telephones just a month before, I used to think "how long until that will be me?" and now another milestone had been reached. I think I had a reasonable excuse to be a little bit excited by it.

Because of the interviewing, I missed an appointment that I had made with Lishanshan, but in the end it didn't matter because she had been dragged into a meeting as well. Hers was rather more serious than mine, being a "Party" meeting. I wanted to ask her about it, but was nervous lest that was the sort of thing that she would become shady about. I am sure that they are not supposed to tell foreigners what goes on.

"Oh! So boring!" she sighed, and I thought that it might be a way to avoid talking about it. But she went on: "It is all about university policy on students, about when they must go to bed, about class times, about *boring boring* things. But luckily there are forty people in the meeting, so I go to the back and can fall asleep and no on will notice." She smiled naughtily, and I thought that she was telling the truth. I found it amusing that young members of the sinister and powerful organisation that is the Chinese Communist Party sneak to the back and fall asleep at its meetings.

Chapter 43

On the train down to Dalian, I was tired and moody, and just wanted to sleep. However, my fellow passengers were more than usually keen on talking, and were full of the most moronic questions. After discovering that I was English, an argument erupted. One of them wanted to know the English for "niu rou." I didn't tell them at once, but allowed the argument to rage. The man nearest to me was convinced that it was "niu rou" in English as well; why would it be different? It just *is* niu rou. It couldn't be called anything else. Eventually they asked me what it was.

"Beef," I said, bluntly.

"Ah!" said the niu rou man, "he doesn't understand. But I promise you, it *is* niu rou." I was happy to be out of the conversation, and didn't try to correct him again.

One of the women at the far end of the carriage had a tiny child in an orange tracksuit. Initially, he was petrified of me, and hid whenever I walked past. I tried to smile in a friendly way and presently his fear turned to fascination. Eventually, he plucked up the courage to ask his older and bolder friend to ask me where I was from. Once he found out, he transformed from a slightly strange but rather sweet little child, into Satan himself.

"Younguoren! Youngouren!" he chanted, mispronouncing my nationality at the top of his squeaky little voice. He jumped up and down, he pointed, and he rushed around, always chanting these grating three syllables. How the rest of the carriage put up with this is a mystery to me, but how I managed to control myself is even more so. At one point, he came within inches of my face with his dirty little finger, jabbing it at me aggressively and screaming. But for a lingering apathy in my muscles, he could have been flung out of the window in a trice, and I would have been in rather a lot of trouble. He was recalled occasionally by his mother, not to be scolded, but to be fed with more sweets. Each time he would come back with higher sugar levels and so greater hyperactivity. Each time he became more insufferable. He crept up behind me and started punching my back. He thrust himself between me and my book and started pinching my arm – really quite hard. All the time I quietly told him to go away. I have never been a big one for disciplining other people's children (and having none of my own, I am utterly unpractised at any form of disciplining), and with the mother so seemingly indifferent to her child's horrifying behaviour, I was at a loss as to what to do. Eventually the elderly man on the bottom bunk exploded onto the little beast, scolding him loudly and waggling his finger in a threatening manner. Incurring the old man's displeasure had an immediate effect on the mother who flew as though on wings to retrieve her beastly little treasure. At last I was allowed some peace. I thanked the old man and watched as the child was stuffed with yet more sweets. I hoped that it would hurt when his teeth rotted out.

Dalian is a great city. Although few people in the West have ever heard of it, it is one of the richest and most loved cities in China. It sits on a mountainous peninsular jutting out into the yellow sea; it is the northernmost ice-free port in China, and consequently was of huge strategic importance in colonial times. There are, by Northern China's admittedly low standards, some quite nice beaches. The city itself is slick and modern, full of five star hotels and trendy (ish) nightclubs. I felt like a provincial bumpkin taking his first visit to the big city. Weaving through the crowds of mini-skirt wearing teenagers that thronged the Friday night streets, I stared up at the shining sky scrapers, and wondered again how on Earth I was supposed to "discover the real China," when it contained such completely and totally different places as Dalian and Qiqihaer, let alone Dalian and Yi Tu Li He.

I spent three days in Dalian, pottering from beach to beach, from bar to bar; shell-shocked by the sophistication, feeling more alien than ever, but understanding for the first time the idea of a city "having a buzz." I had always been told that Shanghai had a "buzz," but had never really understood what it meant. Now, coming from Qiqihaer, Dalian really seemed to be a city on the make: a city where anything might be accomplished, where, with the right idea, the right scheme, dreams could be realised; millions could be made overnight. My travels through Inner Mongolia and Heilongjiang made me feel that I was seeing Dalian as the provincial Chinese might see it: and it was a thrilling site.

However, I found that after this sojourn of excitement and modernity, I was happier than ever to return to Qiqihaer. I found the low rise skyline comforting, and I enjoyed watching the horse drawn carts ambling down the high street. The evening that I arrived back, I strolled around Labour Lake as the sun set. I sat down at the top of the new amphitheatre where middle aged couples were waltzing to Chinese folk music, and looked out across the city. As the light faded, a hotel on the far side began to let off intermittent fireworks, and gradually, as it became really dark, green floodlights were turned on to light up the trees around the lake. In spite of the concrete and the cranes, it was strangely beautiful. In Qiqihaer I never felt the loneliness or the excitement of the traveller any more. As I sat watching the waltzing couples, I slowly began to realise the reason for this change: whilst once Qiqihaer had just been a cold and unfriendly concrete wilderness, and later, returning from Inner Mongolia, it had signified the bright lights of civilization, now, at last, it was home.

www.ingramcontent.com/pod-product-compliance
Ingram Content Group UK Ltd.
Pitfield, Milton Keynes, MK11 3LW, UK
UKHW012217240726
13966UKWH00003B/815

9 781411 671461